Days of Wonder

A Memoir of Growing Up

Bill Vossler

Bill Vossler Books

Dedicated to my patient and incredibly helpful writer-wife, Nikki Rajala, whose philosophies, copy-editing, and reviewing skills helped me get the manuscript right.

Also, many thanks go out to my friends who were kind enough to take time to read this book in advance and make most-helpful comments – Wayne Backman, Burt DuBow, Larry Grossman, Gene Kiffmeyer, Jean Leiran, and Barry Radin. Thanks to each of them.

Thanks also to Executive Editor of the *St. Cloud Times* newspaper, John Bodette, for allowing me to use pieces in this book that had been printed in the newspaper under his watch.

Contents

Return To Wishek

Our Second House

The Empty Lot

Third House, Second Dad

School Tightrope

Seeking Refuge

Church and Religion

Potatoes

Ervin and Baseball

Beastly Learning

The Rest of the Stories

Foreword

Six million years ago a meteor slashed through the eternal darkness of outer space and crashed into the moon. Today, scientists say, the moon still vibrates from the impact.

So with our lives. As we grew up, encounters powerful as meteors flashed out of the dark randomness of life, smashing into our psyches, blindsiding us. The ensuing shocks of pain reverberated in us, followed by aftershocks of confusion that unsteadied us then, and affect us even today.

My childhood conformed to that pattern, amidst the everlasting search for my long-lost father, along with other dark songs of love gone awry: the theft of a horse by my grandfather and the aftermath of his ransacked farm while he was in prison; the first time my POW father died; enduring the intrigues of Apocalypse Granny; our church's wild Old Prayer, and the repeated messages about how I would go to hell, among them.

And yet these pages contain hymns of joy sung in my life during an era of innocence incomprehensible today: discovering dinosaur bones in the empty lot across the street; building our own baseball stadium; my friendship with Ervin, 24 years older and mentally marooned forever at age twelve; and finding freedom during my daily paper route.

Time and order in this memoir may be occasionally jumbled – I might be four, then twelve, nine, seven – because telling the stories of my life thematically ("Bizarre History", "Seeking Refuge", "Learning from Beasts") worked better than simply chronologically.

These stories are rendered as faithfully as I could from my flawed perspective as a growing-up boy, charting the emotional weather of my soul, stumbling in darkness. The Great Silence of my people, the Germans from Russia, who never ever told stories from their pasts left a number of narratives incomplete. However, I completed those stories the best I could, though some won't agree with my conclusions.

6

Fragments of My Life

The First Time My Father Died

The first time my father died, I was but a mote of starlight hurtling earthward from a far-flung galaxy. The twin desperadoes of the Great Depression and drought were squeezing McIntosh County, N. D. in its clutches, wringing out the juices from farmers, including my poor grandparents.

Pillows of sand piled around fence posts, and sifted onto windowsills, seeping into the houses. The stiff whirrs of shiny grasshopper wings filled the air, harbingers of a future of squirming layers of two-inch locusts.

In 1930 when my father, Julius Vossler, was eleven, his sometimes task was to watch the whiskey still. Inevitably he tasted the hootch, liked the taste and the feelings that swept over him, and by evening his soul had wandered into a distant black realm where his return was not guaranteed.

The doctor, thumping Julius' chest and slapping his pale cheeks could not rouse him. *"Er ist dodt,"* (he is dead.)

The doctor smoothed Julius' death certificate, which crackled. He snapped his black bag shut. People jumped. The doctor said, *"Alkoholvergiftung."* (Alcohol poisoning.)

In the creeping darkness the prairie croakers and crickets serenaded Julius' death, their soft songs sifting through the screens, while the sniffling Vosslers grimly stretched the boy's body on a pine board on the parlor table.

His mother Christina felt the implied criticism of allowing an eleven-year-old to watch the whiskey still without supervision. Sighing, hours later she entered the silent house, stepping softly to tearfully gaze at the body of her little boy.

And screamed. Julius was sitting up on the pine board, pale and sick, clutching his head with both hands, his first monster hangover.

Many adventures occurred on Main Street.

John Ackerman, Savior

When I was five, Mom and I were shopping in the Red Owl store. I strayed from her warm hand toward crates of bananas piled against the wall. In one, the slow beckoning of large hairy fingers of a spider drew me. *Come. Make contact.* As I reached out to stroke the big spider, a strong hand grabbed my arm.

"Hey there, young man," a warm male voice said. "What are you doing?"

He seemed a mirage, dressed in blue hat, blue tie, blue suit coat, blue slacks. He pulled out a pen from his suit coat pocket and thrust it into the crate. Crunch! The hairy fingers of the spider grappled at it, wriggling.

He wiped the end of his pen on a blue handkerchief, and knelt, his kind face close to mine. "Hello, little boy. What's your name?"

I held my breath. A man paying special attention to me! Tendrils of aftershave drifted around me. I wanted to hug him.

"What's your name?" he said again.

His gentleness, so different from other distant men in my life, overwhelmed me. I sensed he was unlike the harsher

8

storekeepers, who barked at me for my curiosity, or our minister whose eyes flashed like lightning bolts amidst his sharp words. But this man ruffling my hair was not like them. I gazed into his gentle blue eyes, saw his wide smile, and fell in love.

Maybe he would be my father! I opened my mouth to ask, but could not speak. He might say no.

"What's your name, son?"

"There you are," Mom said. "I see you're in capable hands. John, thanks for watching him. He's so curious. He likes to run around. This is Billy," Mom said, patting my head. I plunged my face into her skirt.

The man said, "Well, Billy. Let's try again."

His tenderness disarmed me so I didn't resist when he turned me around to face him, and tapped my chest. "What's your name?"

I stuck my fingers in my mouth. He asked again.

"Biw-wy," I said, through my fingers.

"Billy? Billy? I heard that Billy has been a really good little boy."

I flushed with pleasure. He asked my age. I mumbled "Five."

"Only five?" He said. "Goodness, but you look older. Let me see your muscles." He felt my biceps, and jerked his hand back in astonishment. "Boy, I wouldn't ever want to fight with you," he said. "That's for sure."

I could hardly bear to look at him, I was so happy.

"Now what's my name?"

I shrugged.

"You don't know my name? Why everybody knows who I am. I'm John." He grabbed my hand and poked it against his chest, leaving a wet spot on his tie. "John Ackerman," he said,. "Say 'John'"?

"J-John."

"That's right!" He squeezed my hand. "John. Good!"

I smiled, and hid in Mom's skirts again.

"Now you remember that," he said.

Never before had I received such kind attention from a man. I froze. What if I never saw him again?

I needn't have worried. He seemed to find me, and every time his eyes focused on me with a vivid blue flame that made me feel that I was the only person in his world, and we repeated the ritual. "What's your name? How old are you? What's my name? Good. Remember that."

Every time, his gentleness touched me, and his smile lay like a warm arm across my shoulder. His calling my name bolstered my sense of self, and I felt happy for days afterwards.

The last time I saw John Ackerman, he was elderly. He tottered up, held my face between his hands, and said softly, "What's your name?" and we played our parts, two grown men chuckling and misty-eyed. "Now don't you forget it!" he admonished me happily as he walked away, and again I felt the warmth of his affection.

I regret that I never said to him, "John, I won't ever forget you, or your name, because you made a little boy without a father feel important by the repeated incantation of my name."

Meeting Daddy Again

One snowy morning with the sky gray as stone, I was on my way to school, slogging through thick new drifts of snow on the unplowed street. I dragged my feet, plowing a path, that I pretended would lead me back home to safety after school. Like Hansel and Gretel in the forest.

I was engrossed in my make-believe worlds, having already been chased by a dinosaur, discovered pirate treasure, and flown up high to view the white world below, when a dark blue car puttered past me from behind. Through the half-frosted window, the driver stared at me. The vehicle slowed, its tires squeaking in the snow.

At the end of the block its brake lights winked on, and the car U-turned. I checked the trail behind me, satisfied no dinosaurs were following. When I turned back, the tires squeaked as the car braked a few feet away. The engine purred and the fan whirred and my heart hammered in my chest as I gazed into the driver's dark brown eyes, eyes identical to mine in the bathroom mirror.

I tried to yell "Daddy!" But all the words in the world broke loose and slid down from my brain, clogging my throat. "Daddy!" I wanted to cry, "Why did you leave me? What did I do wrong? Why don't you love me any more? Are you back to stay?"

Instead I trembled, gray puffs blooming from my lips. Daddy honked. I leaped, and a dam holding back my great river of grief burst, and I began to cry, deep, wracking sobs that shuddered my small frame.

The window rattled as he rolled it down. Warm air and stale smoke and a sharp sour smell enveloped me.

"Billy?" The man said.

I wanted to leap through the window into his arms, but I was paralyzed by the immensity of the moment. He was back after being gone for three long years!

Julius Vossler just after joining the U.S. Army

"Daddy?" I finally said, hoarsely. My heart, though clutched by pain, swelled with happiness. I'd prayed he would return home to me. I'd dreamt of his return. Invented stories of his return. My prayers had finally been answered!

He reached out the window and ruffled my hair beneath my hood. I felt delirious with happiness at his touch. Yet confused.

Why hadn't he returned earlier? Or written? Or called? Had he been sick? I bet he'd been wounded in the war and couldn't return until now!

Maybe he would stay. Oh, how I hoped so!

His eyes darted around nervously. "What grade are you in?"

"What–what?" I said.

"What grade are you in?"

"I-I'm in second grade. In the school. Over there." I pointed at the white stucco building a block away and said my teacher's name.

"That's nice," he said. "Um, how do you like school?"

"It's good. Except David Schmitt always beats me."

"Beats you? Have you told your teacher?"

"No, I just have to work harder at flashcards."

"Flashcards?"

"Yeah, he always wins."

"Oh, I see."

Finally I blurted, "Daddy, where...where...?"

A woman sitting close to him leaned her head and whispered in his ear. He nodded and interrupted. "What do you want for Christmas, Billy?" he asked.

"You, Daddy," I wanted to cry, "You! That's all I want for Christmas. You!"

But the words jumbled together again before they reached my lips, clashing and clanging and melting into tears that squeezed out from my eyes in a torrent.

"A sled?" He suggested, his smile wavering as I continued to cry. "A baseball glove? A ball?"

I thought of my hero, the Lone Ranger. "H-holster," I said wiping my tears with the back of my glove. My nose ran. Snow began to fall harder, filling the air, blotting out the school building.

"A holster?"

"A-a two-gun holster set like the Lone Ranger."

He nodded. "Two-gun holster set like the Lone Ranger. Where should I put it?" When I said white cabinet downstairs, he said, "Sure, I can do that."

He ruffled my hair again, dislodging my hood. Sleet, pellets of cold steel, battered my warm ears.

13

"Daddy, when..." I asked.

He interrupted again and said the weather was turning bad, and they had to get going if they were going to make it home. The car slid into gear. Daddy stuck his hand out. "Here's a quarter. Buy yourself an ice cream cone."

Our hands touched and an electric current sizzled between us for a second. He jerked his hand back. "I don't want to make you late for school, and we have to go."

He rolled up his window. The engine roared. The snow squeaked under the tires. The car drove away. No goodbye. No I'll miss you. Nothing. Except pain.

I stood in a fog of snow and emotion. Pellets ticked off my parka. At the end of the block the taillights lit up red, and then flickered out. Like my hopes. The car turned right on Highway 13.

Breaking out of my stupor, I screamed, "Daddy! Don't go!" I ran as hard as I could to the highway, slipping in the snow, and falling down. As I pushed myself up, I saw the car disappear behind the white curtain. I screeched, "Daddy!" then louder and louder, "Daddy! Daddy! Come back! Don't leave me!"

Too late. I stood crying, but the car did not return. My father drove away into the great sea of life, leaving me floundering in deep water, attempting to rise to the surface and breathe.

I cried the rest of the way to school, realizing no amount of my willpower could ever bring him back to me.

Living With His Loss

Time after time I had imagined that when my father returned, we would walk the streets of life together, hand in hand, instead of me facing life alone. He would smile and hug me and kiss me and say how much he had missed me. Loved me. Put his arm around my shoulder. Read fairy tales to me like Mom did. Show that he cared.

Instead, during his short visit he had never offered a single word of sorrow. No remorse. Instead of acting like a father, he acted like a stranger who happened to possess the same brown eyes, and the same last name and same blood.

In a daze I wandered aimlessly in the schoolyard, punching tracks back and forth in the pristine snow for ten minutes, lost and troubled. The snow crunched under my feet and the cold wind slapped my face, but I felt only numbness.

Finally I pulled open the heavy front door and went inside. When I stepped into my classroom, everyone looked surprised. Deeply befuddled as I was, to me the room seemed an alien landscape.

Where did I sit? One seat near the back of the room was empty. I walked to the chair and sat down. Everybody stared at me.

The teacher said I should take off my wraps. I stood and she removed my mittens and parka. She took them from me and hung them in the cloakroom.

Though I knew I was in the classroom, I fathomed nothing but my father's soft voice and the warm air wafting over my face from the open window. I examined my hand, hoping to repeat the electric sizzle that had passed between us. I remembered the flare of red brake lights, and the car moving away into the falling snow. And realizing that he had left once more, and I might never see him again. I stifled my sobs with the back of my hand. As I attempted to work, I saw I had snapped my pencil point, and I was carving deep scratches in my paper. Like those in my broken heart.

The teacher gazed at me off and on, frowning, especially when I didn't react to the class singing "Billy Boy." Usually I felt embarrassed as classmates smiled at me as the words rose and fell, "*Oh where have you been, charming Billy? 'I have been to seek a wife, she's the joy of my life, she's a young thing, and cannot leave her mother...*'"

At the end of the day, the teacher pulled me aside and asked if I was okay. Tears filled my eyes at her tender concern. Why couldn't my father have shown some? I nodded, donned my winter clothes and began walking home.

Near where Daddy's car had stopped, I paused, closing my eyes, trying to create a happier ending. A car beeped, and hope rose in my heart. I whirled, ready to cry, "Daddy! You're back!" But the car was red, and I jumped as it swerved around me. Had I dreamed the entire episode?

At home I told Mom that Daddy had stopped me on the way to school that morning.

"Ach," Mom said. "You were dreaming. It's another one of your stories."

When I cried, Mom studied me curiously. Then I remembered the quarter. I dug in my pocket. Nothing! I patted other pockets. Nothing! Could I have lost it? Now she would never believe me!

I checked one last pocket. There! I grabbed it and pulled it out. "See!" I cried triumphantly.

Mom blanched. "Where – did you get–find that?"

"Daddy gave it to me," I said.

"Ach, no!" Mom said without conviction.

"He did. He told me to buy an ice cream cone."

Mom examined the quarter. "I lost one and you found it." She gave it back. "Finders keepers, losers weepers."

That ended that.

Except every day for weeks afterwards, I stole down into the basement, flung open the door to the white cabinet, and searched for the Lone Ranger's two-gun holster set. The cabinet remained empty. At times I flopped down on the basement floor, and sobbed, just as empty.

The Story Gene

The mysterious labyrinths in the private universe of my brain are populated by hidden stories that leap from the darkness into the bright light of my imagination to tell their tales. Unbidden, they appear in great detail, triggered by either mundane events or unusual occurrences, creating anecdotes while I'm talking, reading, looking, thinking – living. They project film footage on the theater screen of my imagination, often with dialogue or other sounds, stories about me, or others I know, or made-up strangers.

For example, hearing the clip-clop of the horses' hooves of Ted Boschee's dray wagon finds me riding a white horse alongside the Lone Ranger, humming the 1812 Overture; seeing someone standing at the railing of a ship suddenly creates the story of him leaning over the railing to better see an orange lifesaver with a person in it, and toppling overboard, screaming all the way down; or seeing two strangers behind a window gesturing at each other invents a scenario of a fight and I mentally hear them yelling, he crying that she is working too hard and is neglecting him.

Anything can trigger the stories: the smell and crackle of burning leaves, the blaring siren of a fire truck, or meeting a man walking two dogs in the dark. No rhyme or reason. Sometimes dozens a day, they are the side effects of my being alive. I have little control over them.

I don't know why this happens; a story gene perhaps? Maybe a shard of my imagination broke loose and stabbed into my consciousness, opening a portal to allow the stories to continue? This gift has been part of my life forever.

Stories created in my dream factory vary from a few seconds to a couple of dozen. If they are too painful, I can abort them, as seeing someone I love plunge over a cliff, or get shot. I'll yell, "No, no, no!" But mostly, integral as they are to my life, I don't always realize I'm in the middle of one until it's over and I find myself back in reality.

The Shoemaker

Mom dropped coins into my palm and told me to get my shoes resoled by the town shoemaker, a half block away. I was six and had never had money of my own or bought anything before, so I kept poking the coins in my hand to see if they were real. Excited, I clutched them in my fist and walked carefully to Jacob Rattei's shop. As I turned the doorknob, the door opened from the inside.

"*Komm reigh*," Jacob Rattei said. (Come in.) I followed him into the room, dark as when Mom and I had been there before, with strategically-placed lights off except above his lasts, metal forms shaped like a human foot, holding the shoes he was working on.

Rattei looked like a white-haired god with a pointy jaw. He wore a leather apron from neck to knee. I happily inhaled the smells of leather and leather-soap and other wonderful scents. He pointed me to a chair where I sat and removed my shoes.

He returned to the shoe on the last, pounding nails into a new heel with his leatherworking hammer. Finished, he manipulated the heel, nodding in satisfaction as he set the shoe beside its mate.

He took my shoes, turning them over and examining the flopping soles while he shook his head, saying "Ai yi yi," clucking about *fadumpta* (doggone) kids who were so hard on shoes, so they had to be fixed, which their mother could not afford.

I swung my feet back and forth and watched him as I had when I was there with Mom. He was the first expert I had ever seen, and I was mesmerized by his sure-handedness. He removed my worn loose soles, and snapped open a folded piece of thick cream-colored leather, adding to the smells. The unfolded piece resembled a world map, continents of leather surrounded by holes of shoe-shaped islands and great oceanic gaps where swaths of leather had been removed.

He laid the leather on a table, set my shoes on a continent, drew a grease pencil off his ear, and ran it around the soles' edges. He grabbed a scissors, squinted at the grease line, and a few grunts later, a sole the size of my shoe plopped down onto the table. Then a second one.

He slid my pair onto shoe lasts and with a small brush spread glistening pungent glue on the bottoms of the shoes. Squinting through his thick glasses, he fitted the newly-cut leather on the shoes and pressed it down with his palm, grunting "Ah." He laid a weight on each new sole. He turned to a sewing machine and set it whirring on another project.

Later, he removed the weights from my shoes. He plucked a nail from a picket fence of them between his lips, and with a small flashing hammer tapped the brads into the edges of the sole, one by one, first one shoe, then the other. He thrust his beefy hand inside and felt for protruding nail points. He pursed his lips, turned the shoe upside down, and pressing it against his chest, used a curved knife to trim off slivers of extra sole leather.

He flicked a switch at his workbench, and pressed the edge of the new sole against the whirling wire wheel, smoothing the rough spots. The motor labored as the smell of hot leather drifted through the room.

Finally he held up each shoe, turning it around and around, and with a smile, slipped them on my feet and tightened the laces. As he rose, he slapped the shoes. "*Goot* (good) as new!"

I stood, gazing happily at the new shoes on my feet. He cleared his throat. I opened my hand.

He sighed, shaking his head, gazing at the meager coins shining in my palm. He grunted and said, "*Genau richtig!*" (Just right!) "*Gooden dach.*" (Good day.)

I headed home with my new shoes, my mind reeling with new stories from having seen the wonderful world of grown-up expert work. I felt like I'd been handed a gift, almost as wonderful as the stories Mom read from the *Big Book of Fairy Tales*.

Morning of the Neanderthal

One Saturday morning when I was ten, I was seeking sanctuary from Mom's slaving ways. I had to somehow escape her clutches and make it into the pigweed forest, inhaling the earthy smell of the soil, and listening to the gurgling of the stream in the ravine, before heading to Raile Equipment a block away to watch the Lone Ranger on TV – if no adult changed the channel.

So unless I wanted to be imprisoned all morning, I had to break away. I began loading my mental escape bullets to fire at Mom, but I was too late. She outdrew me, handing me a broom and dustpan and leading me down into the basement.

"Your cousins are coming tomorrow, so I want this all shipshape," she said, sweeping her arm across the game room. But I knew she also meant the other five rooms of torture – the furnace room, our bedroom, the freezer room, the rec room with the model train, and the bathroom.

I tried to protest, but she went on. "No stamp collection, or steelie baseball game or reading or anything else. No distractions of any kind, understand? Just get it done. Then you can go out, or play with stamps."

I sighed, firing my only remaining bullet. "But my hay fever."

"Ach, hay fever," she said, shaking her head.

She didn't believe me. My rap sheet of attempting to avoid work was long and varied, and made me suspect. She thought I was faking the burning eyes and runny nose and sneezing and sneezing.

So I acted diligent. I lifted the big oval rug onto the organ bench, scattered handfuls of maroon sweeping compound, and swept the dark tile floor. I pushed a pile of the debris into the dust pan, sneezing and coughing. I stopped and blew my nose. My handkerchief was soaked. I had to get out into the fresh air. Somehow.

I groaned as Mom watched me dust the model train and table, resetting misaligned tracks and replacing derailed cars, picking out pieces of debris from the tracks, sneezing as more dust rose into the air. I never played with the train. Why did I have to clean it?

Then I spotted my chance: that large oval brown rug. Mom always carried it outside to shake.

I grabbed it, and said, "I'll shake it." Mom frowned, doubt clouding her eyes, doubtless wondering if this was my Escape 101.

Before Mom could react, I said, "Be right back," and pounded up the stairs, dragging the rug thumping behind me. Sneezing again.

I hoped that while I was upstairs, Mom and Ron would finish tidying and cleaning the furnace room, or returning tools to their proper places, or changing bed sheets and pillowcases in our basement room, or cleaning the bathroom, before I returned. Anything would be one fewer chore for me.

Out on the front steps I closed my eyes and inhaled the sweet deep breath of clean air. I snapped the rug, then stopped. The world had been transformed by a swath of fog. Not a normal blanket, but a thick gray five-foot quilt of low-lying fog blotting out the ground. Most of the grain elevators and the upper halves of the houses and the blacksmith shop remained clearly visible.

I took another deep breath and smiled. I loved the great silence of fog. The gray apparition ignited the fires in the mysterious warrens of my imagination, erasing all time and opening a door into the past to allow the shadowy shapes of my mental creations, faint and fine as ancient dust, to step forth.

A block and a half away, the Soo Line train had disgorged its noisy milling human freight. I snapped the rug a couple more times, tiny rocks flying away amidst a small cloud of dust. I stopped again. As I gazed at the fog, a bizarre scene unfolded, a dozen heads of railway workers

21

without bodies moved above the shoulder-high fog. The heads bobbed up and down, with shoulders occasionally appearing, head, shoulders, head, shoulders, as they moved past Scharf's Blacksmith Shop.

I was enchanted. "Wow!" I said. "Wow!" A horde of men seemed to be sliding through the mists of time into the present, heading toward mysterious places.

Then one head broke away from the group and crossed into the far corner of the empty lot. When a breeze thinned the fog, I saw his wide sloping muscular shoulders. They swayed side to side as he shambled through the tendrils of fog in the empty lot. The mist thickened, showing only his head and shoulders bobbing, moving in my general direction.

A breeze thinned the haze once more, so I glimpsed his hairy arms, long and thick so his fingers nearly dragged on the ground. My mouth dropped open. A Neanderthal! I was shocked. I'd seen illustrations of their hairy forms with sloped shoulders and long, thick arms with fingers that nearly touched the ground. Sure enough. Just like this guy!

I gasped. I shook my head, but the Neanderthal remained. The real thing! A live Neanderthal!

I dropped the rug and ran inside. "Ron!" I cried, "There's a Neanderthal coming! Hurry!"

I almost banged into Mom, bearing the rug beater. "What are you yelling about?"

"An ancient man, a Neanderthal. Out there. Come look. Where's Ron?"

Mom grabbed my arm. "Ach, let him alone, or the work will never get done."

"But the Neanderthal…"

"What are you talking about?"

"Out there. Come on." We stepped outside. "Look. There!" I pointed. He was across the street. I gripped Mom's arm. Were we in danger?

As though the Neanderthal had heard me, he removed his cap, and dabbed his dome with a handkerchief.

"Ach," Mom said, "don't be so silly. That's no

Neanderthal. That's Andy Stockburger, home from working on the railroad. He lives up there." She pointed up the street. "Here." She handed me the rug beater. "Grab the rug and beat it good, and get back downstairs. There's work to be done."

"He's real!" I said. "Look."

Mom shook her head and turned toward the basement. "Hurry up now."

I watched the Neanderthal shuffle closer. He stepped onto the road. He smiled and waved, wiping his shiny head once more.

"Just think," I whispered, "A real Neanderthal. Isn't it great?"

"Ach," Mom said. "Don't be so silly. You're just trying to waste time making up your stories. I told you, he's no Neanderthal. Now get back to work."

I paused for a moment as I watched the Neanderthal slouch up the hill away from us, wobbling from side to side. Heading home to chip some flint tools, I figured.

If it hadn't been for my sneezing, I would have missed it. Lucky Mom had forced me to work in the basement!

The Land In Me

Magnify the curled ribbon of my DNA and you will find molecules of earth: grains of loam, courtesy of my German ancestors farming their fields during the late Middle Ages; flecks of silt from the century my people spent on the steppes of the Ukraine; specks of soil from the farms of my grandparents on the great plains of North Dakota.

I was shaped by the prairie. When troubled as a child, I instinctively turned to the land for relief. Like a honking goose winging south, I heeded my instinct, and turned to the land to remove the emotional thorns embedded in my psyche.

I moved through the meadows north of town, or the empty lot across the street, or slid into the ravine where I sat on the ground and leaned back against the wall, tears running down my face while my pants dampened from the soggy sand. I didn't care. I wanted to feel bad, because my father's rejection meant I was rotten, unworthy of being loved.

Here in this land my poise crumpled; here the true tenor of my heart rang out its wounded cry.

I sobbed, wondering how to fill the aching hollowness in my chest. Shortly nature's beauty in the land began to unravel my cocoon of self-pity.

My shoulders stopped heaving as I was enticed by the wonders all about me: layers of soil on the water-cut wall exposing colorful rocks, and ancient dinosaur fossils (so I thought); the gentle smell of the pink prairie rose and the golden triumph of dancing dandelions; the buzz of flying grasshoppers, and scurrying of black-striped curious gophers.

While viewing these glories, the land informed me that I would live my growing-up days without a father to teach me how to play sports, or talk to girls, or navigate life's turmoils. No father to encourage me or praise me when I did well, or gently tell me when I did wrong, and how to do right; no father to share the intimacies of life with. I would have to make do with a mother, grandparents — and the earth.

Jail Time

The year I turned eleven, Easter proved to be a momentous day. My stepfather had finished the house addition, so all my cousins were coming to get a look at it.

Mom was a frenzied *hausfrau,* cleaning with abandon, forcing us boys to spruce up the basement, where we and the cousins would congregate all day. All that remained was food, and I was to help Mom carry groceries home.

I glowed in Mom's attention as we walked two and a half blocks to Herr Mercantile Store. The uptown streets were bustling with last-minute shoppers. Inside the store, the smell of ham and smoked sausage permeated the air.

As we strolled through the aisles, my eyes fell on a jar of silver cake sprinkles. I'd first eaten those BB-sized candies on a piece of cake at a birthday party. When the person sitting beside me left the table momentarily, I gouged some of his out of his cake until it had craters like the moon, and ate them too, much to his dismay.

In Herr's, I let Mom walk ahead. I grabbed the bottle, the cake sprinkles rattling against the glass. The sound thrilled me, which alarmed me and made me study Mom to see if she'd heard. I weighed the cool bottle in my palm, glanced at her, hesitated, looked around, then shoved it in my jacket pocket alongside my gloves. I felt pleased.

Until I met her eyes. I blanched and broke out in a sweat. She always saw through me. Instead she said, "You're flushed and sweating. Are you OK?" She felt my forehead.

"Just excited. About everybody coming for Easter."

The credit book for our family slid down the wire in a small box from upstairs to the checkout, where the clerk found the booklet, opened to a new page, wrote the amount, and had Mom sign the slip. Our groceries were bagged.

As we were ready to head out into the cold, I yanked at my gloves in my pocket. They resisted. I jerked hard, and immediately realized my mistake. But too late.

The bottle of sprinkles leaped out of my pocket, clinking, screaming, 'Help! Help! Look! Look! Thief! Thief!" The eyes of every customer on both levels of the store seemed fixed on me as the bottle smacked the edge of the counter, bounced, making the clicking sound that had earlier pleased me. The jar dropped to the floor and shattered, scattering millions of silver balls in every direction, beneath the wheels of carts, under moving shoes and overshoes, against the bottom of the counter, a great winking tide, and finally stopped. Like my heart.

Mom stared at me with horror. "What are those?" she demanded. "Why were they in your pocket?" She blinked, comprehension dawning, her face a mask of pain.

In a low voice, she spoke to the checkout woman, and asked for a broom. While foot traffic poured around me, I swept up the silver balls and shards of glass, which, by the look on Mom's face, were pieces of her heart.

On the walk home, Mom said nothing, so I concentrated on missing the cracks in the sidewalk with each step.

The next day was Easter. The silence continued. After I set the table, Mom banished me to sit on the bench behind the table, facing the door. "No reading, coins, stamps, nothing. Just sit there," she said.

As our relatives arrived, Mom greeted them, and a pointed at me and said, "Billy stole from Herr's yesterday."

The heavens cracked wide open, dumping shock and surprise in my lap. I hung my head to hide my hot tears. I sat there seemingly forever as each new family was told, "Billy stole from the store."

My aunts and uncles clucked, shaking their heads. My cousins grinned, whispering. Mom looked disappointed and sad.

I ate in silence, and finally my trial ended. Afterwards with a wail I fled downstairs to our room and closed the door and lay on the bed. While I heard our cousins playing in the next room, I pondered the unspoken lesson I had learned: *No son of mine steals. A son of mine is honest.*

Trio of Light Shows

Out through the dining room window, darkness crouched like a living thing until I spotted tiny flickering lights in the far corner of the empty lot. I determined to investigate the fireflies.

"Ach," Mom said, "investigate what? They're just fireflies. And," she added, "it's dark out. You might get hurt."

"But I deliver papers every dark winter morning."

She relented. "Well, at least take a flashlight.".

I found a Ball jar with a cover, punched nail holes in it, and stepped out where the dark night, black and silent as a cave, caressed me. But not total blackness, as outdoors darkness was its own kingdom with its own laws. Above me flowed a spectacular light show that I rarely saw: the gauzy gray band of the Milky Way splashing a spray of a million tiny white stars across the center of the black firmament, with bright beacons of larger ethereal worlds scattered amidst it, the North Star, Big Dipper, and others. Some looked like crystals with light frozen inside.

Overwhelmed, I stood rooted by the glory of the stars, realizing for the first time what "infinity" meant. I felt small and vulnerable beneath the sky's presence, enfolded in its soft dark embrace. I crossed the street into the empty lot, reveling in the spectacle in the cooling night air. To preserve my night vision, I kept the flashlight off, half-stumbling on the uneven ground as I moved into the *marravarich* (stink-weed) patch, where the plants scraped against my jeans, producing a strong smell of sage.

I stopped once more, overcome by a second heaven two hundred feet ahead, winking fireflies imitating the blinking stars. The fireflies winked greenish, or yellow or rare flashing red while the stars above shone white or yellow.

My eyes flitted back and forth, up and down. My heart was filled with the glory of possessing my own colored dancing star-world across the street from our house!

27

Having a dozen fireflies in the Ball jar on the dresser in our basement room would gladden my heart, watching them flicker on and off each night until I fell asleep.

By the pungent odor of water and dead plants I knew I was nearing the pond in the corner of the empty lot. I'd catch heck if I returned with wet and muddy shoes. With one eye closed, I switched on the flashlight. I was safe, a dozen feet from the squishiness, so I turned off the flashlight to gather my prey, keeping my lighted eye momentarily closed.

I'd caught three fireflies with the lid loosely clamped on top when a car appeared across the street, headlights shining brightly. Suddenly fireflies caught in the glare disappeared. Quit flashing. Here one moment, gone the next. Dozens went dark and stayed dark, a third fewer.

Did the headlights herald an enemy to the fireflies? Or too-great competition with a pair of giant fireflies, so they switched off? The car motored away, and when the dark grew again, fewer lit fireflies darted around.

I peered at my prisoners, seeing them flash on and off. How did they shine? Were their butts electric? I smiled.

I snared a few more, accidentally squashing a couple between the lid and rim of the jar. A few minutes later, more fireflies showed up, as the switched-off blinkers switched back on, and I had captured enough. My jar glowed.

I flicked on the flashlight and bathed several flying fireflies in the bright beam. Several went dark. Curious.

Out of the corner of my eyes I spotted waves of color moving in the sky. Here was another spectacular light show, pulsing fingers of the northern lights, thrusting up from the horizon, a throbbing green arc, lighter on top and darker beneath, with a finger of red in the middle. As the colors seeped across the sky, they created abstract paintings in the dark firmament, blending into maroon and red and blue and green hues, making impossible ghostly designs that snatched my breath away.

For a couple of minutes I watched in awe. Realizing Mom would worry, I headed home. As I neared the pool with winking fireflies above, I stopped to examine my captives. They were responsible for my joy tonight. Overcome by the gifts I'd received because of them, I hesitated, then opened the lid and freed them.

Then I received one more gift. The sharp arc of yellow moon quivered on the surface of the pool reflecting the orb rising in the eastern sky. I reached up, imagining I could pluck the moon and stars out of the sky, and drop them into my Ball jar to light up my room at night.

Later in bed, the visions kept replaying in my brain until I rode the light and drifted off into a contented sleep.

The Magic of Words

Word Haunting

I grew up haunted by words. Not meanings, but the rich finery of their sounds. When I heard certain ones spoken the first time – "rugged" and "smitten" and "Revelation" falling from the lips of adults in church; and "slipper" and "Hansel and Gretel" and "looking-glass" with Mom reading from *The Big Book of Fairy Tales,* I was captivated.

Hearing the words, I clasped them to my chest, and whispered them to joyfully hear their graceful lilts, so lovely and rhythm-filled. I cherished them over and over to myself – "chambermaid" and "conjurer" and "seven-league." Fantastic!

But that love brought challenges. I could not keep them floating alive in the air for more than a couple of seconds, as they burst into nothingness, like soap bubbles. Worse, I couldn't say them aloud any time I wanted, like at school or in church. Once in second grade I was chastised for whispering to a classmate. I whispered, but words meant only for me. I teared up, for my teacher did not love what I loved.

I came to know that these exotic sounds also carried on their backs the weight of meaning. But I was too young and unsophisticated to comprehend. Yet eventually I began to realize that when "Rumplestiltskin" was mentioned, I heard not only the exquisite sounds of the word in the air, and the echo in my brain, but also a mind's eye picture of a small man stomping in anger.

Steadily I learned the new words, joyfully hearing them whispered, or spoken aloud time after time: "murmur," "forbidden," "enchantment."

All those words became branded into my brain as with a hot poker, creating scars over which I could run my fingers and feel and remember those words aloud at any time.

Discovering Another Language

One snowy Saturday afternoon, my cousin Rodney gazed at me across our kitchen table, and cleared his throat. Mom had cracked open a brand-new box of modeling clay to keep us occupied, and placed a protective newspaper on the table to protect the tablecloth, while she and my aunt chatted in the living room.

Bob 6, me 4, and Ron 2, after a year in Wishek, 1950.

I was six. Three years earlier we had left the Billings rimrocks to move back to Wishek without my father.

I had never met Rodney before. We rolled cold clay beneath our palms on the tabletop until the goop warmed up and finally softened. I fumed, irked that my father was not with us, irked at having to play with Rodney, irked that he'd grabbed my red clay, and I was stuck with green. When my clay was soft, I pressed it down on the paper.

Slowly I pulled the clay off, frowning when I saw some of the comic figures reproduced on the clay. Dick Tracy. But different. Odd. My attention jittered between the

31

clay and Rodney's face. I could see by his surprised look that he'd never seen clay copy from a newspaper before either. *"Gookst goodt,"* he said. (Looks good.)

I spotted the difference: Dick Tracy was backwards. Facing the opposite direction. His words too. I blinked.

Rodney made his palm print and fingerprints in the clay, so the spirals showed in the soft surface. *"Messer,"* he said, clearing his throat.

I examined his hands and my hands and didn't really see that they were messy, but I nodded.

He cleared his throat again and said, *"Messer."*

I blinked. "Yeah," I said.

"Messer!" he said, louder.

"What?"

"Geps mir Messer!" He rolled the R's at the end of the words. I had no idea what he was talking about. I shrugged and handed him the empty clay box. He knocked it onto the floor and vaguely pointed in my direction saying, *"Messer!"* again, louder.

I took a deep breath and handed him a new log of yellow clay. He backhanded it onto the floor and lunged across the table, grabbing the knife.

I shoved my chair back and raised my hands. He was going to stab me! I opened my mouth to yell for Mom, but Rodney smiled and waggled the knife and said, *"Messer."*

He pointed at the knife. Did he mean 'knife?'

"Messer."

I nodded, though I couldn't yet comprehend the shared connection between knife and *"Messer."* Had he named the knife *"Messer"* like a dog was named "Fido?"

As we played, sometimes I caught a few words between my aunt and Mom in the next room but didn't understand what they were saying. I knew nothing of language, nor that they were speaking a different one. Or that I was in the middle of a maelstrom of languages that would alter my life forever. A real gift, I was to discover.

Seven Languages

A secret river of languages coursed about me and bore me downstream towards literacy as I grew up, channeling me into what would be the greatest gift of my life, a facility with words, and the ability to write.

After playing clay with Rodney I came to realize that English was not the only language that existed, or the only way to communicate. My ears became attuned to this new language, catching snippets in the Red Owl Store, in church, even snatches in grade school, until I began to understand a few words, and comprehend that English and German variants existed side by side in our culture.

I eventually figured seven different language variants were articulated among the 1,288 people of my small town. Four were common and spoken daily, everywhere in the community – in Herr Mercantile, Wiest Drug, the Farmers' Elevator Co., classrooms, on the school buses, over the telephone, face-to-face.

First was standard English, words I heard regularly at school, and spoke, wrote and studied in my classes.

Second was English with a heavy German accent. Many of my people with that accent pronounced their English words differently not only from English, but also from others speaking English with a German accent, so each individual's language could be a sub-variant.

So the same English word was pronounced in different ways, take "drag" for example, the pronunciations could sound like *drak*, or *trak*, or *traig* or even *trek,* depending on who spoke.

The third variant was the ancient Germans from Russia dialect all the older people in my town spoke, brought over the ocean to America, mostly unchanged since my forebears left Germany in 1763. Maybe ten percent of Wishekite spoke only German, like Grandpa Fetzer, and most everyone younger spoke some of it, too, as well as English..

The Germans from Russia dialect was spoken everywhere within at least a fifty-mile radius of Wishek, so prevalent that out-of-state companies hired salespeople who spoke the dialect to come to our towns to sell to area business people. The dialect popped up in gymnasiums during high school basketball games against towns filled with Germans from Russia, called the "Sauerkraut Curtain."

During a basketball game an opposing player might clap and yell in German, "*Geps mir ball!*" (Give me ball.) High school cheerleaders often cheered in German to distract us, hoping we would miss our free throws, cheering, for example: *Blutvurst, Schwatamauga shpeck shpeck shpeck, Ashley Ashley, veck veck veck.* (Blood sausage, pig rind, fat fat fat, Ashley Ashley, go away go away go away.)

Mixed in were Yiddish words, like *futz* (waste time) *bissel* (little, or little bit,) *hah nu* (well, therefore, and others,) along with some Russian, *yupfoyamut*, an awful swear word about one's mother.

The fourth language variant consisted of English and ancient German mixed together in the same sentence, using "whichever word came easiest," as Mom said.

Nuance did not transfer well from German to English, and since my people's first language was German, their English words tended to come out harsh – for example the concept of "different" in German (*anders*) could come out in English as "stupid", instead of a simple "no," or "never;" or *"Bisch du ferrucht,"* (Are you crazy?) might be used instead of "I don't think so," or "I don't know." Harsher than meant.

The next three language variants were heard sparingly, but influenced my love of language, and increased my facility.

The fifth variant included the haunting prose of the King James Bible, words of such smoothness and grace that I felt holy reading them, enthralled by their rhythms, as in Genesis 1:1-2: *In the beginning God created the heaven and the earth. And the earth was without form, and void; and darkness was upon the face of the deep. And the Spirit of God moved upon the face of the waters.* I felt like weeping with their eloquence.

I could see God's giant hands rolling the earth into a massive ball, and pouring waters into black depths of the ocean. The words filled me with bliss, and peace. If I closed my eyes and tilted my head and listened closely I could hear the quills of the scribes of centuries ago scratching on their hemp paper amidst flickering candles in a cold room in an English castle, their breaths painting white balloons as they throbbed with excitement to pen words of such exquisite glory.

The power of these Old Testament words soothed me, engaging my imagination, especially because they did not chastise me like Grandma Fetzer's verses or those in church, which informed me how wretched I was, and in danger of hell fire and damnation.

By the seventh grade, the splendor of those Biblical words moved me to want to write. I hoped to lay down graceful words like in the King James Bible. Instead I scribbled bad short stories, bad poems, bad writing, trying too hard to duplicate those stirring words.

The sixth language variant appeared in Shakespeare's works, like *Romeo and Juliet*. The music in his writings was undeniable: *From forth the fatal loins of these two foes, a pair of star-cross'd lovers take their life; whose misadventured piteous overthrows do with their death bury their parents' strife.*

The seventh language variant was modern German, as taught in our high school.

With these language variants cascading about me as I grew up, I learned the value of words, and fell in love with filling sentences up with them, attempting to create a sense of majesty and power.

The New Old Country

At first I had no comprehension that the border to the old country ran down the middle of the street between our house and Grandma and Grandpa Fetzer's. So when I kicked stones clattering on the road and stepped across the invisible line for the first time when I was eight, I didn't realize I had just emigrated into another world, *Alte Land*, (old country.) On that side of the border everything remained linked heart and soul to the Ukraine of my grandparents' childhoods and *Das Schvarzes Meer*, (the Black Sea).

Grandpa Fetzer, Wayne, unknown woman, Grandma Fetzer.

In this new *Alte Land*, life metamorphosed, with Grandma and Grandpa wearing old-world clothes, she in a print dress with a shawl or white turban or a babushka-like headscarf tied under her chin, he in a white shirt, worn suit jacket, and short-billed peasant's cap.

On our side of the street we designated trees and flowers and birds by English names. In the other, new, country they were christened in German as *Baums*, *Blooma* and *Fogels*. We were no longer boys, but *Boova*; my coat, or *Mantel*, wasn't laid near the window, but the *Fenschter*.

As we sat to eat, or *fressa*, Grandpa prayed with sincerity in German, and then we passed *Vursht*, or sausage,

Grumberra instead of potatoes, poured *Millich* instead of milk, and stuffed food into our *Gooshes,* instead of mouths. If the weather acted up, with *Blitz* (lightning) someone might say, *Gott im Himmel* (God in heaven) or *Dunnervetter* (thunder weather).

I tasted some of the strange words, pass the *Knipfla* (dumpling) or *geps mir Feffer* (give me pepper) but the words tripped on my lips and raised tolerant laughter.

Thus I learned that all things possessed two different names for the same thing — *schlof* and sleep, *schuffa* and work, *laudich* and tired — ancient German words alongside English ones, as in almost all other houses in town.

The common melange of languages made me hyper-aware of words, the bedrock of language, so I came to love words and language. This was a huge gift — or should I say *Geschenk* — for someone destined to become a writer.

Blunt-Speaking

Most Germans from Russia spoke candidly, even bluntly, in English; for example, one day when a woman in Herr Mercantile Store donned a dress and stood in front of a mirror, she asked Grandma Fetzer, *"Vass denksht?"* (What do you think?)

Grandma said, *"Gookst goodt, bis auf den Buckel im Rücken."* (Looks good, except for the hump on your back.)

Mom had the same tendencies, though not with any viciousness. When visitors arrived unbidden in the evening she met them at the door with, "Come in, come in. When are you leaving?" What she really meant was "How long can you stay?"

Or "Ach, don't be so silly," instead of "No," or "That's not right," or "I don't think so," or "I don't know."

The rough language evolved through a long history of my ancestors being tattered by the jagged edges of life lived in perpetually war-torn Germany of the 1700s, suffering utter poverty; then enduring the grinding years of stripping trees in the forests of Poland; followed by the merciless insertion into Queen Catherine's Ukraine, clashing repeatedly with marauding natives who carried off thousands of the Germans into slavery and slaughter, not to mention skirmishes with weather and locusts, and year after year of crop failures.

Living amidst that harshness for centuries bred straight-forwardness into the language. What was said was exact and necessary, making conversations short and blunt.

As I reproduced that blunt language in this memoir, readers may think my people, and especially my Mother, sound harsh – and they do – but they were not meant to be harsh, and were not harsh people in real life. In truth she and many others were kind and loving and caring, but spoke blunter in her second language, like the people around them as they grew up.

The Town of Silence

"As we grow up, we learn about the events of bygone years," wrote Walter Alvarez. "From parents and relatives we hear the history of our families..."

Maybe in most families. Not mine. Never did my parents, grandparents, or two dozen aunts and uncles, ever pull me aside, drape their arm around my shoulder and say, "When I was a kid...," or "I remember the time...," or "You have to know how the terror famine of 1933 impacted our lives..." Or mention our Germans from Russia heritage (more accurately "Germans from the Ukraine," as that is where they all came from.)

None of my townspeople ever spoke of the past, either. None of the 1,288 Wishekites – most of whom were Germans from Russia with common ancestors from the Ukraine – none ever spoke of days gone by, as though they had never happened. A tight-fitting lid covered the great pot of "events of bygone years," creating an overwhelming silence about the past.

In all of my growing-up years I heard only two stories of the past, the first from my barber, as mentioned in the chapter, "Tarnished Hero". Later from Grandpa Fetzer. At times when I felt harassed with my stepdad yelling, "Sticking your nose in a damn book again all day when there's work to be done!" I wandered over to my Grandpa John Fetzer's backyard and watched as he pedaled his whetstone. I was entranced by the river of sparks cascading onto the grass.

He always clapped me on the shoulder, and said, "Yah, da Billy," his hand lingering warmly on my shoulder for a couple of seconds.

One particular day when I was eleven, he seemed melancholy. He clapped my shoulder in a distracted manner.

Normally after saying hello he returned to sharpening a tool, while I sat on a stump and read in silence. This day he gazed into the distance, heaving a mournful sigh.

I knew enough German to say, *"Vass isht loess, Grossfatter?"* (What is wrong, Grandpa?)

His eyes glistened, and in a quaking voice he said, *"Ach, das Schvarzes Meer! Das Schvarzes Meer!"* (Oh, the Black Sea, the Black Sea.) Tears rolled down his lined cheeks, and he groaned as though his heart was breaking.

His eyes shimmered, and gazing back through the mists of time, he broke the silence, speaking off and on for ten minutes. He spoke of life in the Ukraine. Besides the basic words that I knew: *Mutter, Vater, Bruder, Vasser,* (mother, father, brother, water,) *Schiff, essen, Wetter* (ship, eating, weather,) I couldn't follow his conversation.

A couple of times he gazed at me with a haunted look and said, *"Verstahe?"* (Understand?)

Though I didn't, I nodded, because I thought I might eventually put it all together. And I could see he needed to talk.

At last he wiped his tears away, and said, "Yah, da Billy," with sweetness in his eyes, and clapped me on the shoulder again. He picked up a knife, turned back to the wheel, and pressed the edge, buzzing, against the whetstone.

For a brief moment a river of sparks illuminated the shade where he sat, then winked out.

Ironically, in a town of no stories of the past, the first one told by my barber was a lie, and this second one I couldn't understand.

Bizarre History

Horse Thief

Years later I learned that my Vossler grandparents had been poor, barely able to feed their eight children, which was probably the reason my grandfather Jacob Vossler found himself in front of the judge of County Court at Ashley on charges of horse thievery. Jacob said he hadn't wanted to take the horse, but the demon on his shoulder had ordered him to do so. In German, Jacob said his thirty-seven years had been marred by other calamities forced by his personal demon.

Nevertheless in July 1929 the clerk of court of McIntosh County read aloud: "Complaint: that Jacob J. Vossler did wrongfully, unlawfully, and feloniously take, steal, and otherwise carry away by stealing...one black-faced mare, four years of age, and twelve hundred pounds, of the value of ninety-four dollars. State of North Dakota, plaintiff vs. Jacob J. Vossler, defendant, without counsel. For the purpose of receiving the plea from the defendant:

Q: How much education do you have?

A: Not much.

Q: Can you read and write?

A: Not much.

Q: ...You understand this is quite a serious charge being made against you. You understand that, do you? That you are being charged with stealing a horse.

A: Yes.

Q: That it is a felony, a crime punishable by imprisonment in the state penitentiary, understand?

A: (Long pause) Yes.

Q: Do you want to plead to this information–guilty or not guilty?

A: Oh, I couldn't say I am not guilty.

Q: Do you want to say you are guilty?

A: I will say I am guilty.

Q: You say you are thirty-seven years of age?

A: Yes.

Q: And you've never been arrested or in trouble?

A: Not this kind of trouble.

Q: Well, any kind of trouble?

A: No.

Q: How many children do you have?

A: Eight.

Q: All at home?

A: Yes.

Q: How old is the oldest?

A: Thirteen.

Q: And the youngest?

A: One and a half.

Q: How did you come to take this horse up?

A: It came to my place.

Q: Yes, and you put it in the barn, did you?

A: No, in the pasture.

Q: And two weeks later you sold it?

A: Traded it off.

Q: You knew you was doing wrong, didn't you?

A: Yah.

Q: How?

A: Yah, I guess I did.

Q: Well, don't you know you did?

A: Yes, I did.

Q: Did you know whose horse it was?

A: No.

Q: You have now paid Mr. Herr for the horse?

A: Yes.

Q: How much?

A: Ninety-five dollars.

Q: You wouldn't want your children to steal would you?

A: No."

Mr. Schubeck, state's attorney, speaks at this point: 'I would like to say, sir, that this man is not from a bad family. These people pray not to be led into temptation... He didn't make any provision against temptation as it comes stalking into his yard. He says he has not pursued any evil way by intention. He thinks some evil genius is following him and he is now the pursued and not the pursuer. His crops are still in the field. I would respectfully submit to the court that this man be sentenced as of this date, and the sentence suspended while he is out working, bringing his crops in. We can get bond for him. I recommend leniency in this matter.'

Q: Do you, Mr. Vossler, know of any reason why I shouldn't pronounce sentence at this time?

A: I can't get it.

Q: You don't understand?

A: I can't catch on."

Mr. Schubeck interjects. 'I can have the clerk explain it to him in German.' The clerk explains to Mr. Vossler.

"Clerk: He says he just wants to go bring in his crop.

Court: It will be the judgment of this court that you be confined in the state Penitentiary in Bismarck at hard labor for one year, beginning at noon of this day. Sentence suspended until December 1, providing you put up a bond to be approved by the state's attorney and clerk of district court, and that you appear December 1, for commitment."

Though the episode quoted from McIntosh County records ends there, many questions remain:

The horse belonged to Jacob's neighbor. How could he not recognize it?

To whom did Jacob trade the horse? If, as rumor says, to a band of wandering gypsies, on what was he convicted?

A comment eighty-eight years after the incident added a wrinkle. As a lad, a now-elderly Wishek resident was told, "The Vosslers had no food, so they ate the horse."

Which could have left evidence: the branded hide, distinctive horseshoes, or head, enough to convict Jacob.

43

That the family had to eat a horse indicated that Jacob didn't have money to buy food. So he must have been forced to borrow the $95 ($1340 today) from various people. Which could explain why people flooded the farm when he was imprisoned, and carried away everything of value: machinery, animals, household goods.

Years later a distant relative said, "I know the story is true. I was there. I rolled up the floor rugs and took them."

Wall Street collapsed on October 29, 1929. And the farm economy was seriously depressed, as the Great Depression had begun. Money was scarce, and the pilfered machinery and furniture might bring in a little cash.

Perhaps that thievery explains why Jacob's one-year sentence at hard labor was commuted to four months.

Capitol building burning December 28, 1930

Nine months after Jacob's release, on December 28, 1930, the North Dakota State Capitol building in Bismarck burned down. Tinderbox dry like the land, the edifice was destroyed overnight. The December 3, 2015, edition of *The Bismarck Tribune* said, "The cause of the fire is still unknown. Arson was talked about, but no evidence was found."

Jacob claimed he burned the Capitol building down. Was it braggadocio to offset the humiliation of having been in prison?

Neither Husband Nor Father

As Julius Vossler was growing up, my future father possessed all the makings for a happy and successful life. He and his older brother Ferdinand formed the Vossler boys, making money singing and playing at dances, county fairs, and other venues, and probably competed with Lawrence Welk and his Hotsy-Totsy Boys, or Welk's later Fruit Gum

Mom and Julius on their 1943 wedding day.

Orchestra, (offering a free stick of gum to everyone attending.) The Vossler Boys sang songs like, "John Henry," "Wabash Cannonball," "Darling Corey," "The Yellow Rose of Texas," and "Don't Fence Me In."

They sang in a weekly radio show on KSJB in Jamestown, a one-way drive of ninety miles every Saturday. Ferdinand played guitar and Julius played the ukulele and sang in a pure high tenor.

"Oh yes," Mom said, "he had a wonderful voice."

My Mom, Alma Woehl, a gorgeous young black-haired woman, came in from the farm to attend Wishek High School during the week, and boarded with her brother Otto and his wife, Ella. During Mom's senior year Julius' family moved across the street from Otto's, and soon they began to date.

After graduating, Mom taught country school for two years. When Julius joined the Army, the pair eloped, against the fervent wishes of both families. In 1943 she followed him to Camp Claiborne, Louisiana, and Camp Howze, Texas, for Julius' boot camp and training.

It is unclear whether Julius was an alcoholic by this time, but he had been around plenty of available whiskey the family sold during the Great Depression, and had become partial to it.

Within weeks of Mom's becoming pregnant, Julius' unit was activated, and he was sent into the European theater where his German-language fluency would be useful to question German prisoners.

He did finally return home after the war – with a case of syphilis – which he told Mom he had contracted in a Minneapolis café when he slid onto a warm seat in a booth that had just been vacated. "I believed him," Mom said. "I didn't know any better."

After moving to Billings, Julius again began playing ukulele and guitar and singing in bars in a country western band.

Playing music and singing require attention to nuance and sensitivity, but Julius did not transfer that to his own family. The psychological damage from the war affected him deeply.

He began to slip away from husbandly duties, absenting himself for long periods, drinking too much, yelling and raging at us, and spending the money we needed for food.

One time Mom said she had to borrow green beans from a neighbor, which we ate mashed for ten days straight because Julius hadn't provided us any money. To this day my older brother Bob cannot stand green beans.

Another time Mom received $400 from her parents to buy a refrigerator. Julius grabbed the cash and spent it on himself. One night Mom sought him at a bar to coax him home, finding him eating an inch-thick steak.

Julius, with three little boys at home – four and a half, two and a half, and one – expanded his playing status – to other women.

My mother became suspicious, especially after he returned to the fourplex several times with soot on his arms, and lame excuses about its source. So one day she followed him and watched him enter a tent. Later, after Julius left, Mom returned to the tent. But nobody was there. The canvas place contained a cot, table, chairs, and a stove. The inner walls were covered with soot from the stove, except the canvas by the cot which had been rubbed off.

One afternoon a couple of weeks later Mom took Bob and me to a children's movie at the theater a few blocks from the fourplex, leaving one-year-old Ron with my dad.

Bob and I got squirrelly at the movie, so forty-five minutes later we returned to the apartment, where Mom found Julius in bed with another woman.

Mom screamed at the woman to get out. Mom said, "And I kicked her in the ass for good measure. Then the woman sobbed, 'But you have your boys. I don't have anybody!' So I kicked her in the ass again on the way out."

After that incident, Mom made the difficult decision to divorce him.

When I saw a picture of him for the first time years later, he was crouched on one knee beside three-year-old me, smiling, his hair combed like mine is today, and wearing a gray pin-striped suit like one I bought years later – long before I ever saw the picture.

He looked happy; he didn't look like a man who would run away from his sons and cause them pain. "He loved you," my mother said later.

My brother Ron, after visiting him thirty years after he left us, wrote saying, "It wasn't easy to look at him: at his face, scarred from cancer surgery; at his pained eyes sunk in his stretched, stitched skin. I didn't know what to expect as we walked together along a rain-drenched street to a café, where in a mixture of guilt and fatalism, he rambled about my brothers and me as babies, about how he should have stayed with my mother, about the war and the POW camp, about his eight marriages and the rest of his children – his mind sliding and weaving around in time until I got confused trying to follow it all."

Ron added, "In all his post-war photos you can see his haunted look, like he was running from something. But who can know exactly what it was? Who can know my father's heart? Perhaps, sensing his own damage done to him by life or the war, or both, he thought his children might be better off without him. And afraid of rejection, I never asked him that one important question: why did he abandon his children? Why didn't he come back?"

The third and final time I met him, when I was nine, he was like a bright-colored vase that had faded and been broken into shards which could not be put back together again.

My Father's Absence

Though my father's absence from my life became normal, its effect was not. His betrayal left a great wound that would not heal. From childhood the gap remained open, angry red and oozing, into which people in normal interactions unknowingly plunged a knife, poured acid, or scraped against, re-opening the scab time after time.

Each one hurt. Each one spilled blood: as when friends spoke of their fathers; or I spotted other kids with their dads; or heard of my classmates' experiences with them; or watched TV shows featuring happy families with a smiling father; or saw other Vosslers about town; or found remnants of Julius' life in Mom's sewing box; or myriad ways of living that screamed to me, "You don't have a father."

One day in second grade my teacher began asking students what their fathers did for a living. I trembled, and kept my head down, pretending to print capital letters, praying she wouldn't call on me.

But she didn't notice my body language. "And yours, Billy? What does your daddy do?" Her pen was poised like a spear ready to stab.

I was ashamed. "Um, ah," I stammered, "He-he's lost. We-we don't know where to find him."

"He's lost? Oh," she said, and ashen-faced quickly turned to another student.

My classmates smiled behind their palms, and several snickered. I laid my head on my desk and sobbed, waiting for the taunting to begin. "Crybaby! Billy Vossler is a crybaby! Billy Vossler's daddy is lost. Billy Vossler has no daddy."

Kids can be unintentionally cruel, unschooled in what might be hurtful. Or intentionally cruel, gladly releasing the dogs of war. My classmates could taunted me unmercifully when I was in great distress. To my surprise, they didn't.

The room remained silent, except for the next student talking about his or her father. Hadn't they heard me? I raised my head. Nobody was looking, except a couple of quick glances of pity.

In 1953, a divorce was a big deal. Maybe my classmates' parents had said, "Billy Vossler's daddy left, so be nice to him. Don't say anything about his daddy, okay?"

From then on, when someone spoke about their daddy, a frigid wind blew through me, and I sat rigidly in my desk, like an icicle, afraid if I moved I might crack in half.

Nobody ever asked for details about what happened to my father. To which I didn't have answers. Nor did I ask any classmates about their fathers. Maybe others had lost their fathers, too. Instead I remained silent, lonely, ashamed.

A Great Silence reigned over the subject. Nobody ever spoke of it, including in my immediate orbit — family, relatives, or friends. Even Mom didn't want to be reminded of her choice, and loss and pain. The Great Silence of the Germans from Russia remained powerfully in place.

Tarnished Hero?

One day when I was ten, as the barber cut my hair, he told me about my father's war exploits. He said my father's detail was on their way to blow up an enemy ammo dump when they stumbled into a group of German soldiers. My barber told the story in great detail, which should have made me suspicious. How would he know all that?

He said for soldiers, lights of any form were forbidden for fear that bombers would drop a deadly load. After a few moments in the moonless darkness, Staff Sergeant Julius J. Vossler's fluent German convinced the German soldiers to allow them to pass.

But instead of passing immediately, Julius kept chatting, my barber said, reveling in fooling the Germans. "He was thinking of the astonished looks he would get from his mates in camp. And back home where he could brag about how he had fooled the enemy. And play the hero. I knew your dad, Billy, and he was no hero."

I began to feel uneasy.

The barber said Julius' use of unusual words from ancient German finally caught up with him, so the Americans were exposed and sent to a POW camp. "Your mother got a telegram saying he was missing in action, feared dead."

As the scissors snicked, my barber's chest rose and fell faster and faster against my back. "He talked himself into a year of prison camp. I could give a good goddamn about him, but think of what that man did to your poor mother. And with a year-old baby!"

In the mirror, I saw him shake his head. "And the men he personally sentenced to the pain of that hellhole of a prisoner-of-war camp. For a year, Billy, an entire year. I knew your dad. We double-dated together. He was always a great talker. I don't know why your mother ever married him."

I felt like I had to defend him. I said he had endured eight nightmarish months at the hands of the Nazis, and when he finally came back to Wishek in late 1945, he was a different and a broken man. As I was talking, I could feel my barber breathing hard again.

"How old were you when he abandoned you?"

"Three," I mumbled.

"And you've seen him how many times since?"

I struggled to clear my throat. "Twice," I said in a small voice.

"Uh huh. In how many years?"

"Uh, six, no, seven."

The only sound for a minute was the snipping of the scissors while wisps of hair tumbled off my head onto the cloth covering me.

"Let me tell you something else, Billy. Your dad was an asshole before he went to the war, and he was an asshole when he came back. And don't let anyone tell you any different."

He was quiet for a moment. "You boys are better off without him."

In my entire growing-up years in Wishek, from age three to seventeen, I was only told two stories from the past — and this one, I discovered later, was not true.

War Hero

The true story of my father's war exploits proved considerably different, as I found out years later when my brother Ron shared a 1946 issue of the *Wishek Star* with the headline "POW Tells Own Story," where Julius Vossler detailed fighting to capture St. Die des Vosges and Stiege, France. Julius wrote, "November 29, 1944, we of B Co. of 409 Infantry Regiment were called upon to sneak through German lines and destroy an ammunition dump. Being the only German speaker in my company, my captain ordered me to take the lead. Three men volunteered to go with me."

"We said goodbye to our buddies. I thought we didn't have a chance. So we jumped off, and got to the edge of Schletstad, France."

Instead of imminent danger of death, they were unobserved and "destroyed the ammunition dump without any trouble whatsoever."

Just after midnight they headed back toward their unit. "I contacted my captain and told him the mission was completed. He was a mile away with the rest of the company, a total of 180 men. At 0100 we all joined again."

But the elation was short-lived. "We were ready to sleep when all hell popped loose. The Germans blew the river bridge, isolating us from our tanks for support. Their tanks laid the lead to us. We fought for four hours..."

After four hours of heavy fighting, only seventeen of 180 remained alive. "By 0600 we ran out of ammunition, so there was only one thing left to do: give ourselves up as prisoners of war."

This was second time my father died, as Mom received a telegram informing her that he was missing, and presumed dead. Six weeks later she found out he remained alive, as a prisoner-of-war in a German prison camp.

After capture, the survivors were forced to walk three days and nights, Julius says, with nothing to eat or drink, until they reached Stalag 12A at Leinberg, Germany. "There they interrogated us, took all our clothes away...and tortured me for three hours...because they thought I was a German soldier who had deserted."

"December 21st they put us in box cars, fifty men in each, and took us to Stalag 3B near Furstenberg. We stayed in those cars until December 27th. All we got to eat per man was one-third of a loaf of bread, made of sawdust and spuds, and a little water to drink."

Four hundred prisoners were crowded in unheated barracks where each day they received only two slices of bread and a bowl of carrot soup. "On January 27, 1945, we went on a 150-mile march" (sometimes called the Furstenberg to Luckenwalde death-march.) They passed through Berlin on Hitler Strasse to Stalag 3A at Luckenwalde, where a few days later he and other Americans were tortured once more. When one of the Americans died from the torture, Julius and two others knew if they wanted to survive they had to escape.

They ripped out wires from the barracks wall and strangled two young guards. Using maps and money sent by

Headquarters of Luckenwalde POW camp,
Courtesy of Wikipedia Commons.

MIS-X, a secret U.S. agency, they made their way 430 miles across Germany—a true feat in itself—and into Luxembourg, where they contacted the local underground, who hid them in a root cellar.

For two weeks, a twelve-year-old girl risked her life, and her family's, to bring the escapees food and water, until they could be repatriated back to the Americans.

Return to Wishek

Memories of Father

Bob, Ron, and me, near our Billings fourplex in 1949.

The levees of memories of my father, Julius – which should be overflowing – contain only a thin layer of muddy recollections.

In my first memory I'm standing on the worn linoleum in our Billings, Montana, fourplex in his arms. He kneels, and hugs me from behind. I snuggle into his warm chest. His breath tickles my ear. I luxuriate in his touch, amidst the heady tang of liquor.

He flips a small football into the air, grabs it, and sets it nose down on the linoleum, his finger on top. "Kick," he says urgently. "Billy, kick the ball!"

Afraid I'll kick his hand, so I stare. He flips the ball up again and talks as though he's announcing a real game. His voice rises higher and higher, "*The clock is ticking down the last seconds of the game, fans, no time outs remaining, Billy Vossler barks out the signals, hut hut hut, say hut"* he says to me, and I squeak out the word.

He snatches the football out of the air, sets it on the floor, says *"Billy Vossler eyes the goalposts, the ball is down, he kicks, kick!"* he says. I close my eyes and kick, and he says *"It's up and and and it's good, it's good! Billy wins!"* as the ball knocks Mom's knickknacks off a corner shelf.

My father whoops, and pats me on the back. Mom rushes in and spots pink and yellow flowered shards of painted china from the broken teacup on the floor around the football, and screams. I start crying, and my father hugs me. I feel confused. But loved.

In my second memory Julius, my brothers and I are on the lawn in front of our fourplex. Across the street is Athletic Field, home of the professional Billings Mustangs AAA baseball team.

I hear the resounding cracks of the ball against the bat as the teams take batting practice. When my father is busy with Bob, I step off the curb and stagger across the street to the chain-link fence. I press my face against the cold barrier and clutch it with my hands as I watch bats flashing, white balls flying, enthralled by the movement and sounds.

A couple of minutes later strong hands grab me beneath my arms from behind, and lift me up. I howl and clutch the fence, but Daddy is too strong. I kick and cry while he carries me back across the street. Daddy, the protector.

The third memory occurs after the divorce while he drives us five hundred miles from Billings to Wishek, North Dakota. I am napping in the back seat between my warm brothers and I awaken to a shriek. The car swerves back and forth across the road, gravel clattering on the underside. I stand and grab the top of the front seat with both hands.

Outside the black stream of night rushes by, the yellow cones of our headlights punching into the darkness. My parents grappling, Mom sprawling half across him and half across the steering wheel, grasping it with both hands.

My father mutters about driving us off the road, wanted to kill us.

"Don't," she says, "Julius, don't!"

The car rolls to a halt. The driver side door opens. The interior light bursts on. Daddy steps outside. Cool air washes over me.

The headlights slant out past the dark edge into nothing. Mom sobs. My father puffs his cheeks and blows air. The engine purrs. Saved at the last moment.

Years later I mentioned the incident to Mom. "You couldn't remember that!" She said, her face blanching. "You were too young!"

Divorce Court

Fire was kindled in the stars and brought to Earth when Mom caught my father in bed – their bed – with another woman. Thus in a Montana courtroom in 1949, a stern-faced judge glared at my mother, Alma Vossler, and asked if it was her intention to proceed with divorcing my father.

When she said "Yes," the judge heaved a sigh and crooked his finger at her. "Follow," he said.

They strode down a long cool hall to a large window. He rapped on the glass with the back of his hand, motioning her to look down into the courtyard below, which teemed with men wielding pickaxes, loosening dirt, and shoveling it into wheelbarrows. All the workers wore prison garb. Armed guards surrounded them.

The judge looked at her. "You see those men, Mrs. Vossler?" She nodded. "Convicts, every one, many because they didn't have a father. Mrs. Vossler, your three little boys need their father. If you proceed with your wrongheaded choice to divorce that father, your little boys will end up just like those men down there. In prison." He rapped the window again.

Back in the courtroom the judge smiled. "Now, Mrs. Vossler," he said gravely, folding his hands, "this has all been a big mistake, hasn't it? You don't really mean to go through with this divorce, do you, condemning your three little boys to a lifetime behind bars?"

She wiped her tears, set her chin, and said, "Your honor, my husband… Yes, your honor, I do mean to go through with this divorce."

Gloyna Boova

One day when I was seven, a shrill voice from the forbidden house in Wishek summoned me and my brother as we were bringing bottles of milk home. An old woman in a blue print dress and white shawl leaned against a black railing on the porch and cried out. "*Boova!*" she howled mournfully, beckoning us with her hands. "*Boova. Coom doh a bissel.*" (Boys! Boys, come here a bit.) A man sat in a rocking chair.

She jingled coins in her palm and held them out to us, and seemed so sad that we rushed across the street and up onto the porch, forgetting Mom's warning. We grabbed the money. Money! I'd only ever had a few pennies before. But now! Many coins!

Earlier, Mom had shown us the route to fetch milk from our cousin's cows three blocks away. That day, clutching my left hand and Ron's right one, she had escorted us through a stream of rustling brown leaves on the silent streets until we neared a tiny white house on the opposite side with a porch with a black railing.

Mom squeezed our hands so hard they hurt. "Never go over to that house," she said in a low voice. "Always walk on this side of the street. Never go over there. Never! You understand?"

We nodded. My eyes were wide. Did ogres live there? Or witches like in the fairytales she read to us?

But now they looked like normal people, the woman in her blue dress and the man in a white shirt and brown suspenders. On the porch that witch amazed us, hugging five-year-old Ron, and then me, until I ran out of breath. "Coogies?" she said, "Coogies?"

We said yes. She disappeared inside, and returned with a plate heaped with warm fresh-baked ammonia cookies.

Soon we were sitting on their laps, clutching coins in one hand, stuffing cookies into our mouths with the other, while the couple stared at us with sad brown eyes and clasped their arms desperately around our midriffs. "Bik boyss!" the man said, "Bik boyss!"

With me on his lap and his arms around my waist, the man heaved back and forth in his rocking chair. While the porch boards creaked beneath us, he amazed me by spitting brown gobs without a miss into a brass spittoon several feet away on the floor. He laughed wildly and ruffled my hair. I smiled and leaned back against him, feeling his warm chest, smelling tobacco that reminded me of my father. I smiled. I felt good. I felt loved.

The adults traded us and the woman crushed me to her warm, ample bosom. She moaned, slobbering wet kisses on my cheeks, sobbing, "*Boova, boova, mina gloyna boova.*" (Boys, boys, my little boys.)

Finally, cookie-sated and restless, we wrestled loose. The old woman glanced wildly around, and thrust the plate of cookies at us. Two flew off and shattered into pieces on the porch. When I shook my head the woman grabbed her husband's arm and said shrilly, "*Mehr Gelt, Gelt, schnell, schnell!*" (More money, money, quick, quick!) But we clomped down the steps and ran onto the street.

I glanced back. The woman was leaning heavily against the porch post, her shoulders jerking, shiny trails glistening down her creased cheeks. The man sat stone-still in his rocking chair, staring straight ahead. They seemed shrunken, like flies sucked dry by a spider.

At home, I showed Mom the booty and recounted our adventure. She shrieked, snatched the money, and raced into the bathroom. I heard the coins clatter in the toilet bowl as she flushed. Grim and red-faced, she shook her finger at me. "I said stay away from them! Forget about them!"

She scrubbed our hands and faces with soap, and washed out our mouths. "I told you to stay on the other side of the street!" she said in a dangerous voice. "Don't ever go back there! Forget them!"

I nodded, but I was bewildered because those old people were so loving and kind. After that, each time we went for milk we hurried past on the other side of the street, ignoring that little white house with the black porch railing. But always I peeked, hoping for a glimpse of the old man and woman. I longed to be enveloped by those warm arms, glory in their undivided attention, and devour those cookies.

If they were sitting on the porch, they did not look at us, and moved heavily into the house. They never motioned us over again, and sometime in my childhood they moved away, and the house went empty. And yet the shattered stones of their existence continued to weigh in my memory.

* * * * *

Like a dinosaur bone, the incident was deeply buried, but not gone. Thirty years later I was home visiting, alone with Mom. I sat at the table, and while she worked at the stove, I gazed out the window. My eyes roved across the roof of the chicken coop in the back yard where I hid to avoid the skeins of work that could be laid upon me; to the empty lot across the street where I hunted fossils and grasshoppers; down the street to the old water tower; and finally up the hill to that small house with the black porch railing.

It was empty. *Marravarich* (stinkweed) grew rampant in their yard. The door canted on one hinge. The porch floor had rotted through. The incident with the old couple rushed back with staggering intensity. I saw the old woman's shaking shoulders, the man staring blankly, Mom's grim face. Why was I supposed to forget about them? And who were they?

At first I hesitated asking Mom because like other GfR, she never spoke of the past. But she seemed more receptive than before, so I heaved a deep breath and unearthed that dinosaur bone.

"Whatever happened to that nice old couple who lived up the hill in that little house with the porch?" I asked Mom, who was snipping pieces of *knipfla* (dumpling) for supper. The scissors snicked and the quarter-sized globs of dough sizzled in hot grease.

Mom stiffened, and stopped cutting. "What nice old couple?" she said in a choked voice.

61

"Oh, you know. The ones who gave us money when we brought milk home? The old couple you told me to forget?"

Her face went white, "What do you mean, 'old couple?'"

"Well, maybe they were only in their 50s, but you know how kids think…"

Gruffly she said, "You don't know?"

The silence stretched on. I stared out the window. The clock ticked. Finally I figured, that was that. But I heard her sniffle. When I turned, tears glistened in her eyes, and streaked down her cheeks. In a hoarse whisper she said. "Don't tell me you really don't know."

"Know what?" I added irritably.

But truth had already begun to lay its cold finger on my shoulder. For a moment she kept her eyes closed. Lips trembling, she said in a strangled voice, "They were…that was Jacob and Christina – Vossler." I looked at her blankly. She said, "Your father's…father and mother. Your…grandparents."

"My grandparents," I whispered. Slowly I sank into a chair, head swirling, heart thudding.

"You never knew they were your grandparents?" Mom rasped.

I stormed from the house and sped to the lot where part of their dilapidated house now stood. I parted the waist-high weeds, and there where they had once held me in their arms, I sank to the cold ground and cried. I cried for the love and the lives that had been stolen from me.

Like the Montagues and the Capulets, our families had warred since before my birth. The Vosslers were too wild, the Woehls too pious. So my parents eloped, making both families unhappy. Because my father abandoned us when I was three, these unhappinesses kept the families from associating with each other in any way.

Mom said that after calling us onto their porch, a few days later my Vossler grandparents had tried to see us, coming to our house to take us out for the day. Jacob, in his best Sunday suit and white shirt and tie, looking uncomfortable, and Christina, in her best flower-print dress with a woven white shawl over her gray hair and shoulders, like a Russian *babushka*, hoping to be part of our lives.

But my mother and stepfather in their own anger and hurt, sent them away, and told them never to return.

How the tears must have flooded their eyes as they shuffled back down the sidewalk, their shoulders hunched, wondering what they could do to weather such rejection and pain.

Nothing can remedy the loss of my grandparents in my life. I wonder how they might have affected my life in a positive way, and realize that they have disappeared irretrievably. Forever.

The only photo I have of a Vossler grandparent.

Top of the Telephone Pole

One July 4th when I was five, I saw a teenager on the sidewalk near our first house bending over the concrete. Curious, I walked closer to see what he was doing.

"You're one of those Vossler kids, aren't you?"

I said I was Billy. He said he was Myron Wolff. He scratched a farmer's match against his jeans, and held the flame onto a black pellet on the sidewalk. Gray smoke leaped up, and the pellet crackled and swelled sinuously. I jumped back, my mouth agape.

"Never seen a black snake, have ya, kid?"

I shook my head, trembling with excitement as the black snake came alive, expanding and curling and crawling a few inches down the cement.

It fizzled out. "What about fireworks? Ever seen them?"

I shook my head. "I don't know."

From his pocket he pulled out a cherry-colored ball, like a big marble. I glanced at the black snake. The smell of strange magic hung in the air, like in stories Mom read to us. Was Myron a sorcerer? I wondered if he could mumble words to make the sun dim. I wanted to be like Myron.

"You'll like this," he said holding it out in his palm for me to see. "It's a cherry bomb."

On the sidewalk he placed an empty Van Camp's pork and beans can on it, making sure the fuse poked out.

He scraped a match on his jeans, and stuck the orange flame against the end of the fuse. Fire flared and the fuse hissed, belching white smoke. He turned and ran.

I bent closer, my fingers on the warm rough sidewalk, my nose inches from the pungent flame. I smelled the burning fuse. What would happen next?

"Get back!" Myron yelled. A great shadow blotted out the sun. I was jerked backwards. I screamed! A giant bird had swooped down to carry me away!

64

As I flew back, the cherry bomb exploded in a giant boom. The can shot upwards. Like a colorful stubby rocket, it arced up above a nearby telephone pole.

For a moment the can hung in the sky as though suspended from an invisible hook. And began to fall. Toward the telephone pole. Landed with a clink. Atop the pole. Vibrated, but stayed.

My eyes grew large as dinner plates. So that's what you could do with cherry bombs! "Wow!" I said. "Wowee!"

"Damn!" Myron said admiringly. "Never did that before!"

Then he turned on me. "Billy, you have to get back and stay away when firecrackers are lit. They're dangerous. You could have lost your hearing. Or had your eyes poked out and gone blind, you dumb little shit. Do you understand?"

I just nodded, hardly listening, so stimulated by my new experiences. For the next few days every chance I got I stared at the can up there, replaying its flight. I imagined lighting cherry bombs to blast Van Camp cans up on top of all the telephone poles in town. Then the water tower. Why not?

Maybe even knock blackbirds and sparrows out of the skies, squawking furiously, tumbling in a hail of feathers. I couldn't wait for my own cherry bombs!

But Mom said. "Ach, no. Besides, they're too dangerous. And I wouldn't know where to get them. And we can't afford them."

Each July after that I wondered how long it would be until I could get my own cherry bombs, and duplicate Myron's performance.

Christmas, Alone Again

Mom, me holding Ron's hand, and Bob.

Two years after our father abandoned us, I was five, and a howling blizzard a couple of days before Christmas pinned us in our tiny house. The wind whined like a live beast on the spoor of prey as it moaned around the corners along the narrow siding, snuffling for weaknesses into which it could insert its frigid snout and bluster its -40° wind-chill into the building.

We shivered as chilly air wafted around us, three boys sprawled around Mom on homemade rugs laid over the cold linoleum, courtiers to a queen, who was showing us how to make paper airplanes out of pages ripped from the Sears & Roebuck catalog as we listened to music from some records.

But I was more enthralled with the phonograph machine, more interested in spotting the little people who sang so beautifully from inside it. While listening to the radio I'd glimpsed them, but they disappeared quickly, and I hadn't seen any of them with the records.

"Ach, there are no little people singing," Mom said.

I wasn't so sure, listening to "Rudolph, the Red-Nosed Reindeer" and "Silent Night" that emanated from the speaker.

From time to time Mom trudged into the basement, and moments later we heard the clunks of chunks of coal, the clank of the furnace door, and her steps plodding back upstairs to us.

"Ai yi yi," she said. "*Ich weis nit.*" (I don't know.) Her fingers were blackened, and her frown grew deeper. "Uncle Henry can't bring more coal," she said. "The blizzard…"

She brushed a strand of loose hair out of her eyes, smearing a black stain across her forehead. She seemed worried, sighing and wiping her eyes.

But I was happy. We had her all to ourselves, a rare gift. I loved blizzards because we might get to light candles and sit while their flickering glow reflected off our shining eyes while Mom read to us from the *Big Book of Fairy Tales*. I hoped that would happen.

I asked if Daddy was coming for Christmas, but Mom said no. I cried. I wanted to be hugged by him.

She read "Aladdin's Magic Carpet" to us. As I listened, I imagined the rug beneath me gently lifting me and propelling me out into the barren white landscape, empty and cold like my heart. I soared high across the vast dangerous spaces to my father's house.

When the magic carpet landed, I pounded on his door. Daddy pulled it open. His eyes widened in surprise, and his smile spread ear to ear. "Billy!" He cried, hugging and kissing me. "Billy!"

My daydream was shattered by the sad and lovely strains of the record, singing "Don't Fence Me In"": "*Oh, give*

67

me land, lots of land under starry skies above, don't fence me in. Let me ride through the wide open country that I love, don't fence me in."

A moment later the player dropped a new record down, and a man began singing. "Who is that?" I asked. The beautiful voice moved me, and tugged at something inside me.

Mom closed her eyes. "That's, that's Julius," she said. "Your father. He and his older brother Ferdinand used to sing songs like this on KSJB radio, and one time they cut a record, that record," she pointed to the turntable, "with some of his favorite songs." She said he had also sung backup for Tennessee Ernie Ford, who I didn't know. "He also liked the song, 'Bimbo.'"

I knew the words: *"Bimbo, Bimbo, whatcha gonna do-ee-oh, Bimbo, Bimbo, where ya gonna go-ee-oh, Bimbo, Bimbo, does your mamma know, you're going down the road to see a little girl-ee-oh."*

Her lips trembled. As the music faded, snow pellets riding blasts of wind rattled against the windows, and a man with the pure tenor voice, my father, sang 'The Yellow Rose of Texas: *"She cried so when I left her, it like to broke my heart, and if I ever find her, we nevermore will part."*

Ferdinand and Julius played and sang as the Vossler boys.

As the words fluttered in the room, Mom heaved a quivering breath. At *"But the Yellow Rose of Texas is the only girl for me,"* she buried her face in her hands.

I jumped up, scattering catalog pages and paper airplanes, and stood beside her, mute with pain. What had I done wrong? I said, "Mama, Mama, don't cry!" With a great shudder, I suddenly realized why she was crying: she knew I wanted to see my daddy! I already knew such a thing was wrong, and *verboten.* (Forbidden.)

"Mama!" I wailed. She fled into the bathroom, and closed the door. I waited outside, whimpering.

A few moments later, her black hair brushed back, she emerged with red-rimmed eyes. Before I could say I was sorry, she wordlessly pulled me and my brothers into a fierce crushing embrace, kissing us over and over again. In a hoarse voice she said, "I will always love you," she said. "I will never leave you," she said. "Never forget that."

We had no Christmas tree, so Mom said we should imagine one setting on the floor next to the window. After a while I tired of imagining it, so I drew a big Christmas tree in the window frost.

Mom smiled. "Now we don't have to imagine a tree," she said. My heart felt warm.

We huddled, folding paper airplanes by the hot air grate in the living room, blowing out nice warm air, until the coal burned down. Mom draped a thin bedspread over her shoulders, and covered the doorway with a blanket to keep heat in this room. Her face grew longer and longer.

Later after another trip downstairs she said we were running low on coal so the house might get colder. "Uncle Henry might not be able to bring more to burn in the furnace to keep us warm."

"Why not?" I asked.

"He lives on the farm, and can't get through the blizzard."

A fine spray of snow misted through the windowsill crack. A sheen of water grew on the floor under the window.

"Will Santa come tonight?" I wanted to know. Mom said she wasn't sure because of the bad weather.

"That's what Rudolph's red nose was for, to light the way to help him find places in the blizzard."

Mom said she thought he would try.

We spent the cold night crowded together under the bed covers. Early in the morning we heard the scraping of coal being shoveled down the chute. The blizzard had let up, and Uncle Henry was at work providing us with fuel to provide heat. Our new Santa.

Missing Handbook

The signal fires of my imagination have burned brightly ever since my father abandoned me when I was three. Harry Crews said in **A Childhood: The Biography of a Place**, "I've always thought that because my daddy died before I could ever know him, he became a more formidable memory, a greater influence, and a more palpable presence than if he had lived." That was also true of my father, Julius Vossler. His desertion became a colossus creating a massive shadow out of which I could never step.

Losing him altered my life forever, in ways obviously negative, but in at least one massively positive way – his disappearance provided me with a most glorious gift: a powerful imagination.

Because I wanted him back so desperately, my imagination remained constantly in high gear as I continually made up new stories about him. With no pictures of him in our house, I possessed only faint memories of how he moved and smiled. He was a dark and secret river flowing around me towards a strange sea.

Because I could not remember what he looked like, I assembled him as though he was parts of an erector set, took him apart, and reassembled him, related to different scenarios I imagined of his reaction when he saw me: crying my name happily, or crushing me in his arms, or welcoming me with an ear-to-ear smile; or turning away, or telling me to leave, or ignoring me, or saying he didn't want to see me, or he didn't love me. The negative ones were most numerous because he'd already proved them true by leaving.

Each story flexed the muscles of my imagination, strengthening them, intensifying my mind's eye, amplifying my inventiveness, creating a potent dream world, fed by my obsession with him.

Truth is a hard deer to hunt, says Stephen Vincent Benet. Yet no matter how difficult, sometimes you must grasp your weapons, no matter how feeble, and pursue the beast, following faint foot-prints through sometimes-impenetrable jungle paths of the past, hoping to find the prey, or catch a glimpse, no matter how elusive.

Such a search is a solitary affair, for no handbook titled "*Losing Your Father*" exists. No pages on which to scrabble while searching for answers, no checklists down which I could slide my fingers and say, "Aha, I think solution No. 2 works!" Or "No. 6 shows me what to do, and how I should act."

In our small town I knew of no other children who had been abandoned. Nobody told me anything about how to deal with the loss, because nobody knew more than I did. So the guidance I needed did not exist. Meanwhile I clutched a huge balloon of hope, from which I could clearly hear the hiss of escaping gas.

The yearning for his return consumed me, magnified as I tried to understand why he had left me, but worse, why he returned only twice the rest of my life, at ages six and nine. Those episodes elevated my happiness sky-high until he disappeared moments later, crushing my hope both times, destroying me.

As I drifted on the sea of life searching for that undiscoverable longitude where he had disappeared, truths became manifest one by one: he was gone. He would never return. He didn't love me. Never had. In fact, he hated me. Otherwise, why would he have left? It all unhinged me.

Thus I discovered that the delicate strings on which the music of my life was strummed could never again be properly tuned, and were forever doomed to be played off-key. The pained realizations verified Benet's words, *If you eat too much truth at once, you may die of the truth.*

Our Second House

Back of our second house, Bob kneels by Mom, then Ron, Bill, Aunt Minnie, her husband Howard Delzer standing, unknown man on car, with Grandpa Fetzer far in the rear.

A New Life

One spring day when I was six, Mom said we were moving from our first house. I had no way to comprehend how the change would alter my life forever.

Mom grabbed Ron's hand and mine and pulled us toward the front door. Bob followed. "Let's go," she said.

"Where to?" I said. My voice echoed in the empty kitchen. I craned my neck towards a stack of boxes with large words written on their sides.

"Our new house."

I felt excited, but sad. The albatross of loss hung around my neck since my father's abandonment. Losing the

73

house we'd occupied for three years awakened the slumbering feeling of deprivation. "I don't want to go."

"Billy," Mom said, "Come on now."

She led us out. The screen door slammed, punctuating the finality, increasing my sorrow. After moving carefully down the rickety wood steps and cracked sidewalk I turned for a final look. Tatters of paint hung off the siding, windows lacked screens, and scraggles of dead grass pockmarked the yard.

I began to cry, remembering fashioning clay into dinosaurs here, tossing paper airplanes, sorting through physical memories of my father in Mom's wooden sewing box – shiny war bullets, matches, a smooth-sided cigarette lighter. Here I had listened to my father singing songs on the record player. Would I ever hear his voice again?

I stopped, barely able to breathe, feeling Mom's warm hand. "Will-will-will Daddy be there?" I said, "At our new house?"

Mom took a deep breath. "Ach, no," she said. "Come on now." More of my tears flowed.

As we walked in the bright sunshine on the sidewalk along busy Highway 13, my sadness ebbed, replaced with delirious happiness because Mom continued to hold my hand. I didn't care where we went as long as her warm hand clutched mine.

We turned onto a street parading a row of small neat white houses with trees in their yards and boulevards. Chirping birds flitted in the branches, and a woodpecker knocked away at insects that crawled on the bark. The sounds of buzzing insects filled my ears. I breathed deeply of the heavenly smell of flowers from gardens wafting through the air. I had never been in so much of nature's variety before.

I hoped our new yard would have trees and flowers and insects. With no sidewalk, we walked on the gravel street down a gently-sloping-down hill.

"We're getting closer," Mom said.

"This one? That one?"

"You'll see," Mom said.

Ron jerked to a stop. With trembling fingers he pointed at the towering white grain elevator two blocks away. The sharp roof pierced the sky. His jaw dropped. He whispered, "Is that where God lives?"

The top window reflected shards of light. It looked like God's eye! Flocks of pigeons fluttered off the green shingles and circled the elevator. When they landed a moment later they scared aloft half a dozen others. After the half-dozen circled and landed, other pigeons were scared into the air.

"The elevator?" Mom laughed. "No, they store grain there."

But Ron didn't seem sure. Neither was I. Puffy white clouds bumped each other across the great blue sky. Mom clutched our hands as we shuffled, staring at that mysterious house of God. I forgot about our new house.

"Here," Mom said, turning into a narrow gravel driveway between a large two-story house and a small one-story one. I stepped toward the smaller house, but Mom pulled my hand the other way. "No. This one."

"That big one?" I said. "Wow!" Two stories, and three times as big as our first house!

Our new home stood on the corner of a huge lot that stretched all the way to the alley. The gravel in the driveway crunched under our feet as we headed toward the back yard, inhaling new smells.

A large garden of dark earth filled the area. A few dead plants dotted its surface. "No trees," I said. "I want trees like those back there." I pointed toward where we'd come.

"Ach, you'll pass those trees every day going to school, and coming home, and you can go look at them any time you want." Not exactly the same, but okay.

An outdoor toilet stood behind a four-wire clothesline in a narrow slice of grass next to the garden.

"Come here," Mom said, showing us a square of wood. She pulled it up, revealing a rusty pipe wide enough for

75

us to fall into. She said, "I don't want you playing around it, or dropping rocks in. Do you understand?" I nodded. But I thought dropping rocks down into the well to hear them splash sounded like an excellent idea.

A moment later around the back of the house my vision was drawn kitty-corner across the street. I stopped, dumbfounded.

There sprawled four square blocks of an empty lot.

"Look there," Mom said. "You can play over there all you want. Your own playground."

I could hardly talk. "Ooh, wow!" I whispered. I knew she was right. I'd never seen the empty lot before. Yet I felt like I knew it, like I'd spent time in it before – loved this land before.

I felt like this land had been created just for me. The open space spoke to me in the inarticulate gospel of freedom.

Screaming Banshee

One day we three boys were playing in the gravel behind our new second house, pushing blocks of wood with makeshift wheels through the dirt, growling sounds of pretend trucks or cars or tractors. Nearby Mom was scraping weeds from the garden with a hoe.

Suddenly a screaming banshee, her shoes crunching, and wearing Mom's dress raced toward us with a hoe brandished above her head like a club. I spotted a two-foot-long green snake near us.

The Banshee grunted as she viciously swung the hoe, cleaving the snake in half. Again and again she grunted and swung, chopping off another chunk of snake. When the reptile lay in myriad pieces bleeding brown blood, she shoved them away from us with the hoe, as though they remained dangerous.

The attack had been so sudden, and ended so quickly that I hadn't had time to react. My hand still remained on my tractor.

She knelt, gasping, and hugged us. "Are you okay?"

I stared at the twitching chunks of raw meat. Eventually we learned garter snakes were harmless. Made no difference to Mom because she was caring for her children.

Terror in the Dungeon

The basement of our second house filled me with terror from the first moment Mom led us down the steps into the black dungeon with its dirt floor and earthy smell, coal receptacle, furnace, and potato bin. Mom held the door open until we were all in, then stepped inside and released it. The spring on the door slammed it shut into eternal darkness. I trembled and grabbed her leg.

Without windows, the room was filled with an ebony blackness dark as the far side of the moon. A pale thread of outside light at the bottom of the door was eaten up by the gloomy dirt floor. I moaned.

Mom stepped away and pulled the string on the overhead bulb. Light, weak as a bad flashlight, sprayed out.

Trembling, I pointed at the dirt floor under us. "Is hell down there?" I whispered.

She said hell was much farther down, "Besides, we're good Christians, so we are protected."

But from our minister's angry sermons I knew that I wasn't a good Christian or a good boy, so I feared the devils down there were waiting to grab me. I shuddered.

The light bulb hung from a rafter and illumined a small area the size of a refrigerator, which allowed those monsters from hell to lurk unseen in the corners. I shivered in my shoes, and though I was seven, secretly sucked my thumb, hoping Mom would never ask me to go down into that hell-hole alone and bring up potatoes for supper.

A few days later when she said it was my turn to fetch potatoes, I dallied, rolling clay, pressing fingerprints into it and examining the shapes while fear coursed through my veins. I played with the cat. Please don't make me go down there, I thought. Please! I hoped she would forget.

Finally she fixed me with a look. "Go on now."

The basement stairs were in the three-season porch. I stepped out of the kitchen and closed the door, gazing with fear into the dim stairwell toward my doom. I knew each footstep onto the indentations worn into the steps moved me one footfall closer to hell.

Despite the coolness, as I lurched downward I fancied I felt the heat of hell rise up to envelop me. I hesitated on each stair step, slowly sinking closer to perdition. At the bottom I paused, sniffing for sulfur our minister said rose from the fiery pit. I shuddered – I could soon be cast there, the fate of bad little boys, he said, unless they quit sinning, like not listening to their parents, a damning habit of mine.

The blood in my veins quivered when I was confronted by that wide wooden door, portal into the black abyss. I took a quaking breath and leaned against the door, feeling the sharp curls of the rough wood biting my palm.

But felt no heat. The door wasn't even warm. Puzzling. I pressed my ear against the wood, but heard no screeching from the sufferers on the other side.

After what seemed like hours I closed my eyes and screwed up my courage to open the door when I heard the kitchen door scrape. "Billy!" Mom said. "The potatoes!"

Chastised, I heedlessly flung the door open. The spring creaked. I shuddered as dank air smelling of earth flowed darkly around me, absorbing the light. In the dimness I spotted my first goal: the wire hanging from the bare bulb on the rafters halfway across the dirt floor. I had to reach that string and pull it to switch the light on. I swallowed hard. The door felt heavy against my shoulder.

I leaped forward. Before I had run three steps, the door slammed shut behind me. Everything was black and silent as a cave. I was trapped in inky darkness. I could not even see my trembling hand reaching out, grasping for the holy grail of the string. If I could find it within seconds I could yank it. I could flood the basement with life-saving light before the *Menschfresser* (child eater) or demons or other hellish creatures could clutch me in their icy grasps.

Frantically I swept my hand back and forth through the air. I touched the string with my palm! Giddily I grabbed it and jerked. The knot at the bottom snagged against my fingers. The chain rattled against the glass. The bulb flickered into weak incandescence. I dashed deeper into the dim murkiness toward the potato bin. The dancing light from the wildly-swinging bulb leaped against the far wall illuminating a black beast from hell wriggling to free itself from the cement blocks and grab me.

I shrieked. The beast moaned, and began to crawl out, appearing and disappearing with each swing of the light bulb. The hair on the back of my neck stood. My pants grew wet and warm. I yelled again.

With blood thundering in my ears, I grabbed two handsful of potatoes, clutching them against my chest. I turned and raced back toward the door, dropping potatoes on the way. No way was I going to stop and pick them up. I heard the eerie moaning and felt the devil's hot breath on the back of my neck as I raced out and slammed the door. Panting, I leaned heavily against it. Whimpering and groaning. Sounding almost like the monster.

My heart hammered. I pressed my ear against the door. Silence. I was safe! I was about to head up the stairs when I spotted a crack of light at the bottom.

"Oh shit," I said, "no, shit, shit, shit." The light! I had forgotten the light! I would have to go back in and risk my life against the beasts again!

I closed my eyes and leaned my forehead against the door. I didn't dare go upstairs and say to Bob or Ron, "Um, would you go down and switch off the basement light because I'm afraid the monsters will get me?" I would be teased unmercifully.

While I decided my next move, I checked the crotch of my pants. Not as bad as I thought. I could hide it with my hand until it dried. Most had dribbled down sopping my sock.

The light. Leave it on? No, in a day or two when somebody found it lit, they would remember who hadn't turned it off, and I would catch holy hell for wasting electricity and costing us extra money.

I was shaking, and had trouble breathing. If I'd had anything left in my bladder I would have peed my pants again. Why couldn't the bulb just burn out?

I needed a weapon. I laid all the potatoes on a stair, except the heaviest one. It would have to do.

I pressed my ear to the door. No sound. Maybe he'd slid back into the wall?

My mind felt like a heavy stone. I forced myself to grab the door handle. Cold as ice. Took a deep breath. Ripped the door open. Leaped inside. Flung a potato where the monster had attempted to crawl out. The potato smashed against the wall. The door slammed behind me, shocking me. I yelped.

Grabbed the string. Yanked it. The basement plunged into darkness. I turned and ran. Smashed the door open with my shoulder. Picked up all the potatoes. Raced upstairs. Breathlessly handed them to Mom.

"What took you so long?"

I shrugged. "Nothing."

After Ron and Bob went up to bed I told Mom about the monster.

She shook her head. "Ach," she said. "You're dreaming. There aren't any monsters downstairs, otherwise they'd have gotten us already. It's your imagination. Now go up to bed."

Nevertheless I could not stop feeling that if I did not remain vigilant, a monster waited in the far wall to jump out and grab me. Each trip to the basement caused me great anguish. My fears grew larger and larger as I tiptoed down the stairs, ballooning when I opened the door.

One time I opened the door, raced in, and missed the string. The door slammed behind me. I had run too far past the light into the cavernous darkness and couldn't find the string. Supreme blackness enveloped me. In seconds I ran toward where I thought the potato bin was, thankfully bumping it with my thigh, trembling and fumbling at the lumps with my hands.

Unfortunately my fingers sank deep into the gooey core of a rotten one, releasing a stink like an open sewer. I shouted and flipped it away and grabbed other potatoes and turned and ran as though pursued by devils from hell.

Sometimes if I was lucky a feeble orange light glowed behind the grate of the furnace door, or leaped out as the fire roared menacingly, which helped me spot the string. Rather than soothing me, my mind roiled with thoughts of hell's great sulfurous burning fires, the heat increasing as I moved towards the string. Having burned my fingers on a hot pot, I knew the pain the fires of hell would sear across my body.

Though I eventually learned to prop the door open with a chunk of wood, each time I ventured into the basement I remained wracked with fear, doomed to feel as much trepidation as the first time I ever plumbed those depths.

Bob, Ron, and me facing our second house, where mom is taking the picture. Behind us is Walth's house, turret not shown. Behind me is where our third house will be built.

Wet Kittens

One day I heard high-pitched squeaks from under our upstairs bed. I lifted the edge of the quilt, and peered beneath. In the gloom I saw kittens squirming against the mother's stomach. I was excited. I loved cats and kittens! I raced down and told Mom.

She did not seem happy. We lined a cardboard box with rags, and moved the mother and newborns into it. In the porch we set the box next to the basement stairs outside the kitchen door.

Purring, the mother closed her eyes in ecstasy while the kittens palpated by her nipples, sucking out life-giving milk. I picked the babies up, and the mother didn't seem to mind. The little ones squirmed and mewed, mouths gaping until I set them down.

We were in a cold snap, so the porch was cool, which didn't deter me from bringing each of the five kittens into the warm house one at a time, and playing with them. That really irritated Mom. "Close the door! You're letting all the heat out," she said repeatedly.

Then she put the box of cats in the basement, "Where the furnace will keep them warm."

That limited my playing time with them, fearful as I was of that monster-filled arena. I whined about the unfairness, to no avail. "But the monsters might eat them!"

"Ach," Mom said. "There aren't any monsters down there. And monsters don't eat cats."

But if there were no monsters... So the frail babies were forced to endure that scary basement alone. With closed eyes. That troubled me. Remembering the terrifying darkness of the basement, I decided they would not suffer as I had, and would see better in the orange light from the furnace grate if their eyes were open.

So one by one I picked up the warm little bundles and pulled their resistant eyelids open. I had just finished when

Uncle Henry opened the door to the basement, carrying a pail of water.

I should have asked what it was for. Uncle Henry was staying for supper, so Mom asked me to get potatoes for the meal. Despite my trepidation, I felt safer when there was fire in the furnace lighting the basement a bit, which kept the monsters at bay, and I could bring the box of kittens out of the basement and play with them, which I hadn't done all day, because of Uncle Henry's presence.

I took a deep breath, ripped the door open, and rushed in. I smashed into a metal pail with my shins. I tripped on it and struck the ground. Water gushed out. I pushed myself up, feeling something cold and soft and squishy under my palm.

I scrambled to my feet, legs wet and hands muddy. I pulled the light string, turned, and screamed. The kittens! I stepped closer. Inhaled sharply. In my blind haste, I'd squished them!

Four lay streched out by the pail, front paws thrust forward, rear paws backwards, as if running a kitten race on the dirt floor.

Not moving. I'd squished them! Killed them! Every one!

Forgetting monsters, I whimpered and grabbed one and covered its nose with my mouth, gently trying to blow life into its nostrils, as God had done in the Bible. I worked feverishly on one kitten and another and another. They were all cold, lifeless, and wet.

I set the pail up. On the bottom in a couple of inches of water lay a dead kitten, surrounded by loose hairs. I grabbed two of the kittens and ran sobbing upstairs to Mom.

"Ach!" She said, grabbing the dead kittens. She handed them to Henry. "I thought you got rid of them!"

"I did get rid of them. I just didn't bury them yet."

I cried. For a long time afterwards I endured nightmares of the kittens meowing and scratching furiously in the water in the pail.

House of Cards

While in our house with the scary basement, Mom began dating the man next door. Which I didn't know.

I'd met Walter Delzer after a rainstorm while sailing a handmade boat of thin wood in a small stream of water flowing down the hill in the gutter across the street from our house. The clouds had dissipated, the sun shone, and the water ebbed to a trickle so my boat was getting hung up.

I heard footsteps scraping nearer on the sidewalk. Large black shoes stopped. A man's shoes! Daddy!

"Daddy!" I blurted, glancing up, not realizing how prescient my cry would be. I was paralyzed with happiness. The bright sun blinded me, and then realized he wasn't my father. Too tall. Unless he had grown a lot since I saw him last. No. This was a stranger wearing a white cap with paint spots. Tears filled my eyes.

He asked what I was doing. I held up the boat. "Sailing," I sniffled.

He smiled and said his name was Walter and what was my name? I told him and he patted me on the head and said he would see me around. He seemed friendly.

Shockingly, they married and he moved in. Suddenly I had to fight him for Mom's attention. I had been tossed off the deck of a boat in calm waters into a whirlpool sea of change. I didn't want a new father!

One morning two weeks later he and Mom were going to Ashley. Before we left for school, he warned us not to run in the gym during the annual Sauerkraut Day, where we would eat our German meal along with a thousand other people. "*Baus oof*," he said, (Look out) waggling his finger at us, a warning we'd hear many times in the future.

Later that day, he and mom returned. He stomped into the house and pointed a long finger at us. "Why the hell were you guys running in the gym today! I told you not to!"

My jaw dropped. How could he know? He looked at me. "I've got eyes in the back of my head," he said. "I know everything you do!"

For years afterwards I believed him, and tried to spot the eyes through his thick black hair, but never had any luck. I didn't want a new father, so I thought if I irritated him enough maybe he would leave. After he said something at the supper table, I mumbled so he couldn't understand me. That frustrated him. I was angry I wasn't receiving enough attention from Mom, too.

One evening I built a house of playing cards on a small table in the living room. Mom and Walter sat side-by-side on the couch, talking and laughing. I wasn't thrilled with Mom's attention to him, but I was thrilled at my card house growing bigger and bigger, outstripping what I'd ever made.

Slow as the hour hand of a clock, I fitted the last card in place. I dared not breathe until I leaned back, and then only out the side of my mouth. I was afraid to wiggle.

"Mom!" I said urgently. "Look!"

To Walter Mom said, "Just a minute." He frowned.

Walter and Mom after their surprising marriage.

86

I wanted to stay in Mom's spotlight longer, so I had invented a story about Jesus perching on this wonderful tall card house to view all creation.

Mom walked over, and Walter followed. I was surprised but pleased. He moved closer to praise my work. He stared at me with a peculiar glint in his eyes. When he leaned closer I smelled the sharp stain of liquor on his breath.

Before I could begin my Jesus story, Walter swatted my house down. Cards flew. I shrieked, and grabbed his arm.

But he was too strong. He swept the cards onto the carpet. They fluttered around me like red and black pieces of my soul.

I sobbed. Mom was aghast. "Why did you do that?" she said angrily, gazing at him incredulously.

"Billy has to learn that it's a cold and cruel world out there."

At that moment I hated him. I withdrew my sharp saber of words. "My dad is going to get you," I said.

The room grew silent. Behind Walter, Mom leaned off to his side, her finger on her lips, terror in her eyes.

He laughed. "Your worthless dad? Where is he now? Who the hell do you think supports you? Under whose God-damned table are you putting your legs? Who's raising you, for Chrissakes? Me, that's who!" He thumped his chest. "Not your asshole father. He had his chance, and he ran off. Left you. And you ought to God-damn know right now that he's never coming back. Never! Understand?" He turned, then wheeled on me. "I'm your father," he said with emotion in his voice. "And don't you ever forget it."

I slumped down. My father was never coming back. Never! The jagged lightning of truth struck me.

Smothered with grief, I stumbled out of the house, Mom calling behind me. In a blind frenzy I raced across the street into the empty lot, through the stinkweed patch and into the ravine. I crawled down into it, smelling the dank earth, hearing the rush of water, and leaning against the crumbly dirt wall, sobbing until I ran out of tears.

Walter's act destroyed more than just the house of cards. His wanton act destroyed any hope that I could have faith in him and increased my yearning for my absent father.

When Mom turned her attention toward me, he must have felt threatened. Or maybe he had begun to realize he'd taken on more than he bargained for, parenting three little boys of five, seven, nine.

My already-low trust in father figures plummeted as Walter's dagger of betrayal stabbed deep into my psyche, and instinctively I remained wary of him forever. Because I was a child and failed to understand his action, from then on I faced all the men of the world as strangers and adversaries.

The Empty Lot

A Country of My Own

Ron tosses a baseball from in front of the empty lot, with the "Is that where God lives?" elevator behind him.

Blinded by darkness, I nevertheless pressed my nose against the window at the edge of the attic where we boys slept. The land kitty-corner across the street was my land, and I was watching to make sure nobody came at night with lights to steal it in some unnamed way. I felt like it was a privilege to live that close to nature and its extravagant beauty.

The terrain with the powerful-smelling *marravarich* plants, pigweed forest, sometimes-pool, and ravine so thrilled my seven-year-old heart that I assumed the empty lot thrilled other kids too. I feared they would soon overrun this four-square-block expanse in delight, and I would lose it. To keep the place to myself, I determined to keep others out, maybe pound in poles, attach wire to them with signs declaring the land "Billy Vossler's Country, closed to tourists," or

89

proclaiming "Keep Out! Danger!" But where could I get the poles and wire?

However, the problem solved itself. After a couple of weeks of meandering in my new country, immersed in joy, I was shocked to discover my fears were unfounded. Nobody else noticed the empty lot. Nobody crossed its border. Bicycles and cars sped by and nobody glanced at it. Nobody stopped. Nobody except me was interested in the empty lot.

Bliss filled me from toe to top! Gates of happiness swung open. The empty lot was mine!

Two-Mile-High Glacier

The wind moaned, rattling snow against the dining room window. I lifted my eyes from my Indian head penny collection on the table, and gazed across the street into the empty lot where I fancied I spotted the foundation of a modern glacier forming, a buildup of snow now four feet deep. A layer of ice from the pressure of the snow was undoubtedly forming at the bottom. The first of many. The beginning of another glacier. Another ice age!

In school I heard that a continent-sized ice sheet, called the Laurentide Ice Sheet, had covered most of North Dakota some 20,000 years ago. The glacier arose after thousands of years of the earth cooling. Snow fell, rarely melting, piling higher and higher, until it created a great cathedral of ice jutting out of the earth, a two-mile-high glacier whose top was barely visible. On this very land where I was now sitting!

In a book about glaciers I read that those uncountable billions of tons crushed down with unimaginable pressure, squeezing the earth. When the ice grew to about a hundred and sixty feet thick, the weight began nudging the glacier forward, creeping just an inch to a foot per day, but always moving. I loved imagining this ice mountain inching along.

Half the glacier – the top mile – was ice, the other half rubble frozen to the bottom as it scraped its way southward. The glacier dragged all sizes of rocks iced into its underside, some as large as a garage. These boulders scraped dirt and debris loose from the ground, and transported it along, though I was surprised to read that nothing was bulldozed by the front of the glacier. Also that the rocks clutched in the bottom of the glacier etched scratches into boulders in the ground.

While the glacier advanced, the inside remained alive. Rivers of melt water cascaded through interior openings, mixing sand and pebbles and rocks and dropping the aggregate along the way. Thirteen thousand years ago the climate changed. A thousand years after that, the glorious glacier began to die, surrendering to the warmer sun and air, steadily shrinking until it came to nothing.

I learned that the runoff helped create massive Lake Agassiz at the borders of North Dakota and Minnesota, and far up into Canada, 116,000 square miles of glacial water. When the ice melted, the pressed-down land slowly began to rise back up over thousands of years – and is still rising today.

The glacier dropped an unsorted mixture of clay, silt, sand – and boulders around Wishek. This outwash sediment created the landscape, the rolling hills, potholes, moraines, tills, eskers, and broad flat plains. And amidst all that, the empty lot of my youth.

A Learning Ground

When you pry open the earth, unexpected items might leap out and surprise you with gems of discovery. Even stupefy you, as I found while digging in the empty lot.

A pile of dug-up gopher scree exposed a few small white bones. Curious about them, I spaded deeper around the hole, and turned up twenty more. Because they were so small, I figured they were the ribs of a snake.

And then, thud. I struck something solid. I shoveled sand out and in the shadow inside the hole saw a gray rock the size of a large pineapple. With effort I pulled it out. I scraped earth away, and saw that a smooth finger-wide groove ran around the narrow middle. Instantly I knew I'd received an ancient gift – an Indian war club! I whooped with joy.

In a trickle of water in the ravine, amidst the smell of sage, I washed the surface clean. On one end I spotted a streak of long-dried blood. The hair on my neck rose. How many skulls had this weapon crushed, like eggshells? I glanced into the pigweed forest and clutch of *marravarich* nearby, where a brave might be lurking.

I examined the cold rock, the rounded smooth front end, and grunted as I hefted the club and tried to swing it. Took great effort. Hundreds, perhaps thousands, of years ago, the club had been cinched tightly to a thick wooden handle by rawhide thongs wound around the smooth groove. I marveled at the strength the warrior must have possessed to brandish it. The discovery electrified me.

Later I found an inch-long arrowhead, as gorgeous and deadly-looking as the head of a rattlesnake. I imagined a warrior squatting on his haunches in the pigweed forest, feathering a shaft and attaching the arrowhead. Peering out he notched the arrow on his bowstring. He parted the leaves, drew back the string, his biceps bulging, and shot the arrow singing towards a deer. The jolted deer leaped, whirled for a few quick steps, swayed, and crumpled to the ground, dead.

Viewing the colored strata in the walls of the ravine made me think that ancient winds from every direction must have snarled across the plains and raged across this prairie millions of years ago, carrying dirt of many colors from miles away, laying down different-shaded tiers.

When I heard that a massive heavy glacier had once occupied this empty lot, I believed its immense weight pressing on plants must have turned them into coal, then diamonds. Precious valuable diamonds! Certainly the two-mile-high glacier that had once crushed this land down was enough to squeeze out a raft of diamonds! Here was my personal diamond mine! All I had to do was find it.

I told Mom we were going to be rich. "Ach," she said, "don't be silly. There are no diamonds over there. Just a lot of smelly *marravarich*."

So I set out to prove her wrong. I liberated a spoon from the kitchen and scratched out the thin black layers into my hand, searching for the sparkle of diamonds. I poked through the pile of black sediment in my palm, but nothing glittered.

After an hour of digging around, I was puzzled. What was wrong? Nothing was there. Maybe the veins of coal needed to be thicker than a sixteenth of an inch to make diamonds? I was hugely disappointed.

My disappointment didn't last long as I began to discover other hidden treasures in the strata, husks of grasshoppers, bodies of black beetles, a broken turtle shell, agates, round rocks the size of marbles, small bones, long convoluted roots of grasses and bushes, all of which I studied to my heart's delight.

During summers I knelt happily in the ravine, light breezes ruffling my hair, or broiling suns sucking sweat out of me onto my forehead. Nothing except chore time – lots of that – and playing baseball, kept me from my appointed rounds in the ravine.

When Mom missed her spoon, I had to revert to other diggers, stout branches, a blade of my pocket knife which dulled as I dug out and exposed chips of flint, quartz, and other rocks in brown, black, or tan layers. I scraped my fingernails down to nubbins.

One day I sat back in the ravine and realized that no other human in the history of the world had ever before seen these very layers! Wow! That made me feel really special. I shook my head in awe.

My imagination ran amok, creating a fabric of energy out of my thoughts: maybe I could find veins of gold! Or copper! Clubs of ancient cave-dwellers! Teeth of *Tyrannosaurus rex*! Pieces of an *Allosaurus* skull!

While in the ravine, I traveled back into a long-distant ancient world, listening for the rustle of leathery pterodactyl wings overhead, hoping for a glimpse of the long-beaked beast in the blue sky. Or hearing the scream of unfortunate prey as a roaring dinosaur closed in, just around the ravine's curve where I fancied dinosaurs lived.

One time I unearthed six smooth round rocks the size of flat tennis balls, all practically on top of each other. Gizzard stones! Which I had just learned about. They were big, so the beast had to be big. Like a *Brontosaurus*. When I licked one of the rocks, I couldn't taste any stomach acid. I tried another. Just dust. I shrugged.

Nevertheless, I was sure the giant beast must have died here, else why would the gizzard rocks have remained bunched together? And how could the dinosaur have died? I thought for a moment. Killed by *T. rex*, of course!

Suddenly I was mounted on the neck of my pet *Tyrannosaurus rex*, Tyranno, howling like a wild man as we spotted a *Brontosaurus*. I flicked the inch-thick reins to urge Tyranno forward. Ahead the big slow beast spotted us, brayed in fear, its eyes growing huge and white, and rumbled away, flinging up gravel from beneath its feet as it attempted to escape into *marravarich* of the empty lot.

I kicked my mount with my heels. Tyranno roared and glared over his shoulder with an eye larger than a tennis ball, and clacked his yellow teeth big as a picket fence.

I jounced, hard put to stay on his back as his body thumped the ground with each step, talons gouging prints six inches deep into the rain-softened ground, deeper where he lunged and seized his prey's neck with giant knives of teeth.

Bones crunched. The *Brontosaurus* squealed piteously, thrashing for a moment, but soon lay still. Tyranno's roar was muffled as he filled his massive maw with a bloody meat.

Sure! That was how the gizzard stones got there! But where were the fossil bones of the *Brontosaurus*?

After digging and poking around for a couple of days, I came up empty-handed. Nothing resembling bones large or small. A mystery. Probably washed away by an ancient river. I discovered I wanted to know more about these dinosaurs.

They both were much larger than I thought. A *T. rex* fourteen feet at its back, and where I rode on the neck, twenty feet. Forty feet long, weighing 18,000 pounds! Wow!

The *Brontosaurus* was even larger, seventy feet long – almost impossible to believe – and weighing 30,000 pounds! I also found that gizzard stones were called gastroliths.

As winter set in, I heard about Ray Bradbury's short stories about the ancient past, like *A Sound of Thunder*. I was transported back into a steamy Cretaceous jungle with a *Tyrannosaurus* bearing down on me: "Out of the mist, one hundred yards away, came *Tyrannosaurus rex*. It came on great oiled, resilient, striding

Photo taken at Dinosaur World in Kentucky.

legs…a great evil god, folding its delicate watchmaker's claws close to its oily reptilian chest. Each lower leg was a piston, a thousand pounds of white bone, sunk in thick ropes of muscle, sheathed over in a gleam of pebbled skin like the mail of a terrible warrior… And the head itself, a ton of sculptured stone, lifted easily upon the sky. Its mouth gaped, exposing a fence of teeth like daggers. Its eyes rolled, ostrich eggs, empty of all save hunger. It closed its mouth in a death grin… It ran with a gliding ballet step, far too poised and balanced for its ten tons. It moved into a sunlight arena warily, its beautifully reptile hands feeling the air. 'My God!' Eckels twitched his mouth. 'It could reach up and grab the moon. It can't be killed! It *sees* us!'" I was mesmerized.

Another time in the ravine I plucked out a fist-sized rock with a thick inch-long fossil. A shark's tooth? How could that have gotten here? Never an ocean here. Not possible.

But soon I discovered an ocean indeed had existed on this very spot. The melting Laurentide Ice Sheet had filled the central U.S. with a half-mile deep ocean, the Western Interior Seaway, with sixty-foot-long vicious *Mosasaurs*.

So a *Mosasaur* tooth! Even better!

I imagined a beast lurking underwater near the shore of the prehistoric sea waiting for prey. When a *T. rex* wandered down to drink, the *Mosasaur* leaped out, and clamped the dinosaur's snout in its jaws, yanking the beast towards the water. The *T. rex* fought viciously, digging down with its feet, scraping deep talon trails down into the water.

The sea boiled, but the dinosaur had never met an enemy like the *Mosasaur*, and in its element. The gigantic beast crushed the life out of the *T. rex* with its terrifying teeth, and ripped it to pieces, filling the water with clouds of blood.

Mosasaur from Wikipedia Commons.

Dinosaur Mix-Up

Joy pulsed through my veins, ticking in my temples as I stood at the edge of the ravine in the empty lot, clutching a rusty spike in my hand. I was an eleven-year-old dreamer.

I jumped down three feet into the ravine, and stood in the sandy bottom, feeling the land come alive beneath my feet, the earth trembling under the vestiges of the pounding of the great legs of the dinosaur giants who lived here millions of years ago. The wind whispered, echoing the ancient predator roars, wafting primal smells amidst the death cries of prey, and the flapping of leathery wings above.

As my dream faded, in a holy trance I touched the layers of sediment in the ravine where I would surely unearth bones of *Triceratops, Brontosaurus,* and *Tyrannosaurus rex.*

I shook my head to clear it and bent to work, wielding the cold spike in the hot sun, scraping away at the dirt. I was slowed by golden gems of discoveries, agates like ancient amber, and tiny white bones, all of which deserved to be honored, through immediate examination.

Finally I cut my meanderings short. With the rough edges of the rusty spike scraping my palm, I stabbed deep into the base of the side of the ravine, unmasking the aroma of damp jungle earth. I was on the right track!

Later, after many minutes of work, I yelled joyfully as I disinterred my first dinosaur fossil, a two-inch-long tooth of a young *Tyrannosaurus rex.* Then a few minutes later a second one! And a third one that I wasn't sure of, but thought it might be from a *Brontosaurus*. But after another hour, nothing.

Success was fleeting. Digging time was limited by the season, and by my paper route, playing baseball, and whatever Mom assigned – household chores, hoeing, picking potato bugs, working for others. Many sessions I found no fossils. But the dream was hard upon me, and I continued to work it, because sometimes like magic, a piece of fist-sized fossilized dinosaur bone would drop at my feet—a piece of an *Allosaurus* skull bone, *Stegosaurus* tail-bone, and a *Triceratops* horn point. Anyone could see that that's what they were.

But dig hard and deep and hope as I might, the real prizes, the giant bones, eluded me. My tools never clunked onto any deeply-hidden two-or three-foot-long fossil dinosaur bones. Hugely disappointing. I vaguely wondered about borrowing a tractor from the lot of the implement dealer half a block away to excavate tons of dirt to speed up the work and unearth the golden prizes. No matter that I'd never driven a tractor before.

One evening while examining the dozen dinosaur fossils I'd found so far, I turned to the address a teacher had copied down for me – the Smithsonian Institution in Washington, D.C. He said the Smithsonian would examine any fossils I sent, and identify them. Free of charge!

Whoa! I could hardly contain my excitement!

But I was leery. What if these rare and irreplaceable fossils got lost in the mail? What if the Smithsonian stole them from me? "I'm sorry, but we never received any such package from you." But my teacher vouched for them.

And once they were identified, I planned to sell them to museums for big money! Maybe the Smithsonian! Identifying them would help me with my unbelieving classmates, too. "Dinosaurs? This one from the Weenysaurus, huh?" And so on, amidst laughter.

They were just jealous. But when the Smithsonian identified them as dinosaur fossils, I'd have proof positive. And the last laugh!

I wrapped two fossils in newspapers and placed the bundle in a small box. I wasn't going to risk losing all twelve in one fell swoop. But the result looked so pitiful and unimportant that the box could easily be laid aside and lost, or ignored for months. Or years.

Added two more. Still pitiful. Four more. Heck with it. All of them. I asked the Smithsonian to identify the dinosaurs fossils and please return them. Stashed them in a shoebox, and sent it.

99

Afterwards every day was excruciating for me and the post office workers too. "Any packages today?"

"Nope."

"Today?"

"Nope."

Were my fossils so rare the Smithsonian had decided to steal them? Day after day, nothing – until three weeks later, a post office worker, Millie Kautz said, "Billy, are you expecting a package?"

I almost jumped over the counter. "Yes," I said, "Yes!"

"From, let's see, it says here, oh, some Smith?" She was smiling. "Oh, the Smithsonian?"

"Yes!" I screamed, tearing up. I ripped the box open, and inside with fossils was a letter on onionskin paper: It began, "Dear Mr. Vossler," sending a thrill up my spine, *"The identification of the specimens that you sent..."*.

Mr. William Vossler
122 No. 7th St.
Wishek, North Dakota

Dear Mr. Vossler:

    The identifications of the specimens that you sent in are included with the specimens. These are being returned to you under separate cover. When you receive this material, please sign, date, and return the white copy of the invoice in the enclosed envelope which requires no postage.

                    Sincerely yours,

                    C. Lewis Gazin, Curator
                    Division of Vertebrate Paleontology

Enclosures

"Dear Mr. Vossler," Smithsonian Letters began.

Dear Mr. Vossler:

Your request for identification of fossil specimens is hereby acknowledged. I have taken the liberty of numbering them in order to distinguish them and submit the following information:

1-4. Molar teeth of extinct horse, probably Equus complicatus.

5.   Incisor tooth of extinct horse, probably Equus complicatus.

6, 7. Molar teeth of an extinct species of Bison.

8.   Distal end of metapodial, probably horse.

9.   Proximal phalanx, probably horse. Note that number 9 articulates fairly well with number 8.

10.   Distal end of phalanx of horse?

11.   Distal end of metapodial of artiodactyl. Not right for deer, moose, elk or Bison; possibly camel?

12.   Possibly piece of skull of large artiodactyl-like Bison, from frontal region near base of muzzle.

A word of explanation: The metapodial is the foot bone just below the hock, and the phalanges (singular, phalanx) are toe bones. The term distal refers to the end of a single bone, or a bone in a series, farthest from the body.

All of your specimens are from Pleistocene (Ice Age) deposits.

This material is being returned to you under separate cover. When you receive it, please sign, date, and return the white copy of the invoice in the enclosed envelope which requires no postage.

Sincerely yours,

Nicholas Hotton III, Acting Curator
Division of Vertebrate Paleontology

Enclosures

The Smithsonian Institution sent detailed letters back, identifying fossils I'd sent them.

The second page said, "*Your request for identification of fossil specimens is hereby acknowledged. I have numbered them to distinguish them and submit the following information:*"

Could hardly wait. Which were *T. rex*? Breathlessly, I read on.

"*1-4. Molar teeth of an extinct species of Bison.*

5. Incisor tooth of extinct horse, probably equus complicatus.

6, 7. Molar teeth of an extinct species of Bison."

101

Holy mackerel! Those ancient beasts cavorted around the empty lot thousands – maybe millions of years ago! But where were the dinosaur IDs? I ran my finger down, searching for *T. rex*.

"8. Distal end of metapodial, possibly horse.

9. Proximal phalanx, probably horse. Note that number 9 articulates fairly well with number 8."

Same horse! Same leg! Exciting. But where was the information on the dinosaurs I'd sent? Checked again.

"10. Distal end of phalanx of horse?

11. Distal end of metapodial of artiodactyl. Not right for deer, moose, elk or Bison; possibly camel?

12. Possibly piece of skull of large artiodactyl-like Bison, from frontal region near base of muzzle."

I snapped the paper in frustration. No dinosaurs? Impossible! I checked again, with fading hopes. Still nothing. I closed my eyes. All that work, for nothing! Maybe something in the final paragraphs?

"A word of explanation: the metapodial is the foot bone just below the hock, and the phalanges (singular, phalanx) are toe bones. The term distal refers to the end of a single bone, or a bone in a series, farthest from the body. All of your specimens are from Pleistocene (Ice Age) deposits. Please sign, date, and return the white copy of the invoice in the enclosed envelope which requires no postage.

Sincerely yours, Nicholas Hotton III, Acting Curator, Division of Vertebrate Paleontology. Enclosures."

I stared at the letter. After a moment I realized what had happened. A mix-up. They'd sent me the wrong letter. That was it! Somewhere else in the U.S. another kid who'd sent in agates was scratching his head while reading a letter identifying dinosaur fossils, mouth gaping in surprise.

I'd return my letter. Get things straightened out. Then I saw "Dear Mr. Vossler," again, and twelve white numbers on the fossils I'd sent, matching twelve numbers in the letter. I heaved a deep breath. Closed my eyes. Realized I was wrong. Smithsonian hadn't identified dinosaur fossils in my box because there weren't any. I felt like crying.

I was bummed. When I whined to mom that the fossils were only from the Pleistocene Era, she asked what that meant. I didn't know. That helped me regain some confidence. What was the Pleistocene Era, anyway? The encyclopedia informed me that it had begun 2.6 million years ago, as most of the world was being covered with ice – the Laurentide Ice Sheet. The Pleistocene lasted until 11,700 years ago. Holy mackerel!

So I'd found Ice Age fossils. Still ancient. And unique. I swallowed my pride and showed them to classmates, who teased me, "So they aren't dinosaur fossils?" But the Smithsonian words matching fossil numbers – "Distal end of metapodial..." and fossil 8 "articulates fairly well," with fossil 9, convinced them.

The letter spurred me to dig more. What else was hidden in the ravine? Or elsewhere in the empty lot? *Mosasaurs* and *Plesiosaurs* from the ancient sea? Woolly mammoths? Ancient peoples? Dinosaurs? I hadn't given up.

So I sent more fossils to the Smithsonian. The curator must have quailed, "Not *another* box from that boy!"

Each return package contained a letter addressed, "Dear Mr. Vossler," everyone of which still thrilled me.

These wise experts, with enthralling titles like curator, and acting curator of the Division of Vertebrate Paleontology, humbled me as they took time to identify my fossils.

They also kindled a powerful love of archaeology in me. Delirious with excitement, I couldn't wait to dig up more fossils, and show everyone my discoveries.

Exciting Outdoor Experiences

The empty lot provided years of exciting experiences. A few times I floated on a homemade raft on the still waters of the shallow sometimes-pond in the far corner of the lot, dreaming of drifting down a river filled with adventures, free from responsibilities and adults. Huck Finn the second.

Under the hot summer sun the pond disappeared, leaving a shiny mud flat which degraded into hardpan with meandering cracks that formed large brown maps that might have been different countries of the world.

In the empty lot my brother Ron, friends Tom and Ron Klein, and I, fought pitched battles with fistfuls of sharp horsehair seeds that we flung sticking into the enemies' shirts, so we yelled and arched our backs away from the prickling.

In another corner of the empty lot grew a great copse of five-foot-high pigweed plants. The inch-thick plants produced leaves large enough to hide safely under.

Here we fought battles with pigweed rifles, into which we injected pigweed shells, fired, ejected, and reloaded. In that pigweed forest we hunted each other.

One time I searched for my enemy there, walking silently and stealthily, examining the ground for spoor, muddy prints, a dropped pigweed bullet, a broken branch, or other traces big or small.

Kneeling in the coolness while moisture seeped into my pant legs, I inhaled the rich aromas of rotting debris, and the powerful earthy smell of the soil.

I parted the leaves and peered ahead. The silence made me wary. In the muted light that filtered down, I scanned the damp earth for my enemy's footmark.

There! The faint impression of his barefoot heel in the soil. My senses humming, I stooped, my eyes darting side to side. Sweat leaked out of my armpit.

In the heel print the delicate whorls were clearly visible, etched a minute ago. One careless act. His final one.

My knuckles were white on the stock of my pigweed carbine. No birds chirped, no rodents scurried. Even the insects paused from their ceaseless murmuring. Too quiet.

My heart hammered. Slow as an hour hand I turned my head.

A flash of color. A scream. I scrabbled for the pigweed knife in my belt.

Too late.

I was knocked down. The weight of my enemy squashed my shoulder into the damp earth. The edge of his cold knife bit into the soft white underside of my neck. So this is how I would die, flailing in the stench of rotting leaves!

My enemy flung back his shaggy head and laughed, baring his long teeth. "You almost had me, Willy," Tom said. He removed the pigweed knife from my neck. "But you made one mistake." He slid off.

I rubbed my neck. "What's that?"

"The arrowheads in your pocket. I heard them clink together when you moved."

Inside the cool dimness, all my troubles disappeared, the pain of missing my lost father, the tense relationship with my stepdad, the challenges of growing up, were all replaced by the freedom and joy of being in nature.

As the Gregorian wheel of my youth ground down the days of my life, I ran my heedless ways in the empty lot. It was my second classroom. I learned about ancient history from Indian artifacts; the making of rivers from water coursing through the ravine; geology, with the layers in the walls of the ravine; archaeology from the Smithsonian who identified my fossils; flora and fauna, the names of plants and animals; weather and clouds; astronomy, gazing at the bright holes of stars punched in the black firmament; even more, the sense of curiosity, and discovery, and joy.

That empty lot was a microcosm of life; a practice ground for living. This was my turf. I knew it intimately. I loved it unreservedly, this "empty" lot. I was proud of this landscape that bore me along the days of my early life.

105

Woehl relatives by the WPA park building.

The Work of the WPA

When I played in the empty lot across the street, waded in the town swimming pool, ate lunch with relatives in the shelter in the park, I didn't realize I was surrounded by the work of Franklin Delano Roosevelt's WPA, or Works Project Administration. The narrow WPA sidewalk began outside our house across from the empty lot, and traversed ten blocks south through town, ending along the swimming pool. What gifts came from that sidewalk!

On that walkway, ants rushed pell-mell with seeds, grass snippets, feebly moving bugs, and insect corpses five times their size. On that cement path – and on the ants – I learned to perfect my basketball dribble.

The narrowness of the sidewalk forced me to learn to control the ball as I dribbled, or else it would strike the rock wall or boulevard and career off into the street, rolling down fifty feet into the intersection. Hitting moving ants required concentration and skill as the part of the ball that struck the sidewalk – and ant – was minimal. Along the sidewalk in front of our house ran a WPA-built wall, comprised of rocks the size of a man's fist. The wall began as a mere one-footer, then two feet high in front of our house, and three feet in front of Walths, our neighbors. The wall continued up to our garden. No other street in town sported such a wall.

One day in junior high, I was shooting baskets on the gravel court next to the school gymnasium, when the basketball rolled over toward the building twenty feet away.

When I picked up the basketball, I paused, awareness blossoming in my brain. The gymnasium rocks, pinkish, bluish, gray, mirrored the colors of the shards in the rock pile in the center of the empty lot across the street from our house. That pile contained the sliced-off edges of the ones used to build the gymnasium, swimming pool building, and nearby park shelter. These remnants were a foot square, and a foot by eighteen inches, and an inch thick.

The wall clearly tapered in front of our house.

The auditorium was originally built as a Civic Center.

No Desire To Swim

A single glance proved the swimming pool building had been WPA-built of the same colored rocks as the gym.

Because I was afraid of water, Mom signed me up for swimming lessons when I was eleven. The lifeguard handed us some small rocks in waist-high area of the pool, and said we had to learn to keep our eyes open under water. I didn't understand why, but followed directions to drop the rocks.

But when he gave the order to dive and grab the rocks, my willingness ended. I was trembling, remembering how I'd almost drowned because of that man who lied to me about the depth of the lake right off the bank. So no way.

He noticed my hesitation. "Drop them Billy," he said. "Now all of you go down and get them!"

Everybody dived. Except me. I splashed water to seem like I'd dived. I was farthest away from him by the pool wall by the sign spelled "tempature." His eyes weren't on me.

As swimmers surfaced and showed their booty, he praised them. Meanwhile I pushed my rocks against the side of the pool with my foot and scraped them up against the wall, raising them high enough to grab with my hand. Without diving. I showed him the rocks, and perhaps seeing my wet chest, he thought I'd dived. Lucky he didn't check my hair. "Good job, Billy," he said.

I was petrified he knew of my subterfuge and would force me to dive and bring up rocks in front of everybody. But nothing happened. I chose to make that my only lesson.

I encouraged Mom's belief that I was still attending lessons, saying to her each time, "Oops, swimming lessons this morning. Gotta go," and happily clambered onto my bike and headed out – to Wishek Concrete Products and Lumber Co. to climb joyfully over huge piles of rocks searching for fossils, agates or other stones. Or pitching a baseball against the backstop at the diamond. Or playing pinball at the bowling alley downtown – anything but swimming.

Third House, Second Dad

Meeting the Witch

One day while eating dinner, our front door smashed open as if struck with a battering ram. It smacked against the radiator and bounced back, shuddering.

Yeep! I cried, clattering my fork onto my plate and knocking a piece of chicken onto the floor. I slid off the bench and hid behind mom in her chair. I was eight.

At first glance the perpetrator seemed an ugly old woman, like the witch in Hansel and Gretel. But why didn't she call up her magic powers and just walk through the door instead of crashing it open? Maybe to scare us? Mom stayed silent, though she always reprimanded us for making noise when we slammed the door.

I was confused and frightened. Had a witch come to roast me in an oven? I clutched Mom's arm.

The woman stood on our doorstep, wearing a white turban, print dress, and brown stockings that sagged down her ankles. She held an open book in the palm of her hand, and with bright sunlight exploding around her head, she thumped the book with her other hand.

"Es sakst im Bibel," (It says in the Bible,) the interloper croaked.

Her eye sockets were black. With the bright light surrounding her she might have been an angel. But angels were beautiful. And young. And sported wings. Maybe I was wrong. I waited for a heavenly chorus and lightning and thunder and the deep holy voice of God to announce her, as in Bible stories. But nothing heavenly occurred.

"Mommy," I whispered, "is she an angel?" Then I had a terrible thought. "Or the devil!" I whispered. I quivered. But wasn't the devil a man? And no horns.

"Ach no," Mom said, "She's your new grandmother."

"*Grossmutter?*" My new grandmother shrieked. *"Gott im Himmel."* (Grandmother? God in heaven.) "Not as long as the sun shines." Her hand swiped the air, erasing that dark possibility from the blackboard of life.

"But I married your son," Mom said, "So my boys are your..."

She shrieked again, and shook her head. *"Sakst nit. Isht nit"* (Say not. Is not.) "They aren't, for you have made an adulterer of my son in the eyes of the Lord God Almighty."

Flames seemed to leap from her eyes. She pawed ravenously at the onionskin pages of the Bible.

The sun seemed to dim as she stepped forward and fixed Mom with a dark stare. She thumped the book, wailing as she punctuated, *"Es sakst im Bibel."* (It says in the Bible,) '...whosoever marrieth a divorced woman,'" she thumped the Bible harder, "'commits adultery.'" Matthew 5:32. "These are the words of God. *Es sakst im Bibel.* You have made an adulterer of my son."

She clapped the Bible shut with a shot like artillery fire. I jumped. Suddenly the door was empty, and Mom slumped against me and uttered a stifled sob. I was crying too.

Thus Mary Fetzer, purveyor of powerful high drama, was introduced into my life. Though introduced was not the proper word – more like catapulted.

Apocalypse Granny

Each door-clattering visit from Grandma Fetzer filled me with darkness, a descent into the black heart of a mountain. During one incident I jumped in surprise, and screeched, lurching and scraping a crayon line across a drawing of a *Tyrannosaurus rex* fighting a *Triceratops,* ruining my work. Another time I crushed a thin green clay snake I'd rolled out. Yet another I knocked colored stones I was playing with far and wide. Once I nearly stuck my food-filled fork up my nostril. She stunned me each time she appeared.

Thus I kept one eye perpetually on the front door. Waiting. Waiting for the apparition to return.

When would she smack the door open again? And how did she arrive so soundlessly? I never heard her. Never caught the rattle of the door knob. Never saw the knob turn.

But boom! There she was. Maybe she was a witch!

During each episode Grandma presented a three-act play. Act I was Matthew 5:32, reminding us that Mom, a divorced woman, had forced Walter into adultery by marrying her. I did not know what adultery meant, but I knew it was not good.

For Act II, Grandma thrashed at the onionskin pages of the Bible in her palm to find her next favorite part of our household's sermon, from Exodus 34:7: "...The sins of the father are visited upon the child, even unto the third and fourth generations."

Not any generic father, I sensed, but my own unworthy dad. I knew he had sinned grievously, because like a unicorn, he was extinct. No pictures of him. His name was

111

never mentioned. He never visited. As though he was dead. Which in a way he was.

My own sins already weighed heavily on me, dealt out anew during church sermons or songs each Sunday amid phrases like, "a poor wretch like me." I didn't know what wretch meant, either, but hearing it with congregants sobbing aloud during prayer meant it was not good.

Grandma quoting Exodus 34:7 filled me with despair. I trembled facing sins I had inherited from Adam and Eve, and now knowing of the hordes of sins laid on me by my father. And those from his father, and maybe even his father, even unto the third and fourth generations, piling, piling, piling. I felt overwhelmed by my rottenness.

A third act followed, a variation of her favorite theme: the apocalypse; the end of the world was nigh. She rustled through the worn holy pages for verses that reflected her belief, verified by recent world occurrences.

Following an earthquake, she crashed open our door and like a colossus thumped the Bible, saying, *"Et sakst im Bibel,* 'and I beheld when he had opened the sixth seal, and, lo, there was a great earthquake…, Revelation 6:12.'" After a solar eclipse, she rushed over and palming the Bible, said, "'… And the sun became black as sackcloth of hair… Revelation 6:12.'"

When the harvest moon glowed red, she smacked open the door the next day, and pausing in the sunlight, said, *"Ist blude uf der mundt,* (There is blood on the moon.) *Et sakst im Bibel,* '…and the moon into blood, before the great and the terrible day of the Lord come…, Joel 2:31.'"

While I writhed each time, our front door would suddenly stand empty. But my brain was filled with fears that were multiplied by each of her appearances, so I began to hark to the rising of the winds and shattering lightning and pounding thunder, searching for signs in the night stars, feeling for the earth shuddering beneath my feet, or the blinking out of the sun, or blood on the moon. I was convinced that one day Grandma would smash the door open, and stand with her Bible in a light so bright I could not bear to look at it, and usher in the end of the world.

When Mom became pregnant, Grandma's sermons grew fewer and farther between. Grandma had gotten to know us. We butchered chickens, rabbits, and hogs together, planted and harvested potatoes, attended the same church, ate occasional meals with each other – just spending time in each others' presences. So she began to ease up.

When my brother Wayne was born, Grandma's door-crashing episodes ceased, except for rare times when the evidence of the world ending overwhelmed her, and she needed to vent her fears. More often she sat at the table with Mom, discussing the Bible, religion, and life. She cooed over the baby, and chatted, until bit by bit she and Mom grew to be friends.

Yet she remained a mystery. I never overcame my fear that she might still one day begin again to smack the door open and start on a sermon. I hoped not, because after each sermon, it took me long to journey out of the darkness and back into light. She instilled the fear of God in me, convincing me that the Bible verses she read came straight from God.

Though I remained wary of her, I grew to love her as my true grandmother, an ardent, passionate, funny woman who unintentionally mentored me in how to create drama.

Mom , Wayne, 1954

Mom and Grandma became best friends by about 1956.

Grandma Fetzer takes a break from butchering chickens. Uncle Howard Delzer stands by Bob in the baseball uniform, Walter sitting.

Hoena Schlachta

In the early years of our communal chicken butchering, Uncle August Huber deposited crates of squawking birds in our backyard on the day of the *schlachta* (killing).

Later, each spring my brother and I hefted home four-inch-high two-foot square cardboard boxes full of chicks from the post office, or nearby hatchery. On the way we heard their gentle cheeping music, their scratching feet, and felt their soft feathers pressing against our fingers inside the handholds. Air holes in the narrow sides were crammed with probing yellow beaks and downy yellow plumage.

We released the chicks into a side room in the chicken coop where they ran about, shrilling for their lost mothers.

114

They were cute and I could not imagine that we might ever harm them in any way, much less butcher them. I could not equate the little yellow fluff balls to the white feathered fiends we had to watch to keep them from flying over the fence and landing in someone else's pot.

Each year the sounds of footfalls rustling in the autumn leaves cued my family into an orgy of food preparation for the winter. Besides mounding potato bins brimful with spuds, Mom canned beets, cucumbers, green beans, peas, tomatoes and pickled watermelon rinds. When she finished with the hard and hot work in the kitchen, she waited for the jars to cool, and the lids to pop, indicating they were sealed tight. Then she set the filled Mason jars in rows on shelves in the basement.

But the glittering jewel of our food preparation was the assembly-line butchering, or *hoena schlachta*, (chicken killing) of a hundred of the beasts in our backyard. Guts spilled out not only from the fowls, but also words from the fulminations of folks who disagreed, doubly dangerous with their knives flashing around.

The day before, knives were brought to Grandpa Fetzer to sharpen on his whirling whetstone in his backyard. Jars of rubbing alcohol for burning off pin feathers were unearthed from their hiding places, and tables were set up in a basement, or our back yard.

On those butchering days I yearned for freedom while gritting my teeth as my heart teemed with malice toward the stupid beasts. Killing them was sweet revenge, and fun, repayment for the useless hours I'd spent in the blazing summer sun forced to watch them.

In our backyard, a cauldron of water boiled over an open fire, and knives and other needed items lay on the tables with containers for chicken parts of gizzards, livers, and so on. The workers consisted of Mom, Walter, his mother Grandma Fetzer and stepdad Grandpa Fetzer, we three kids, and sometimes other relatives, like Aunt Edna. Other than seeing the chickens react and the chickens dead, I found joy

115

spending time with these people I loved, and feeling like an equal, even if my work methods were criticized.

My first job was to nab chickens. Each one I grabbed protested so loudly that passersby could have been forgiven for believing the bird was being decapitated slowly and painfully. I clamped the chicken's body between my elbow and ribs to still its wings, and learned to grab its legs to prevent scratching from its sharp-nailed toes, and brought the sacrifice to my mother, the executioner. If I placed it at her feet, she stood on its wings, and expertly wielded the large black-handled butcher knife, its edge newly-honed razor-sharp.

Mom grabbed the chicken's head, stretched the neck, and plucked away a few feathers with the knife. The chicken emitted a muffled squawk, silenced by a sharp stroke of the knife through its neck.

Now came my favorite part of butchering chickens – witnessing their bizarre behaviors. When they lost their heads they did not yet realize they were dead. For each cut-off head tossed onto the ground, the membranes over its eyes blinked, the beak opened and closed, and a tiny pinkish tongue poked out. On the decapitated body the white bones of the bare neck were visible and great gobs of blood spurted out.

Sometimes after I carted a live chicken to Mom, I held it beneath my arm while she sawed off its head. Then I "accidentally" dropped the chicken to the ground to create the high point of butchering. I couldn't wait. Headless chickens always seemed to land on their feet and performed one of three antics:

Some stepped forward in a stately walk, spurting crimson fountains of blood in time to the beating of its heart, creating a white-coated *maître d'* with a messy red scarf about its neck. You could almost see the missing head turn disdainfully side to side.

Some of the doomed birds raced into the trees to the side of the chicken coop and banged against the wire fence along the alley, their wings first flapping fast, then slower, and slower, while blood spurted less and less until nothing more came out, and the bird toppled over.

Other chickens hit the ground sprinting full tilt, fluttering wildly, as though they were sure they could change their fate, shouting, "Where's my head? Help! Help! I've lost my head," scampering across the yard and sometimes across the street into the empty lot, as though searching for the missing appendage, leaving trails of blood on the road.

After a couple of minutes of draining, I grabbed the chicken's orange legs and lugged the body, dripping a small trail of blood, to the vat of boiling water. I dunked the headless chicken and held it under until all the feathers were sopped. A powerful stink arose.

I pulled the body out, allowed water to gush out for a moment, and began grabbing clumps of boiling-hot feathers. With my bare hands. I yanked out the sodden masses, my hands burning like fire. Gloves would have remained scalding hot and very wet, and waiting for the water to cool would have made scads of difficult-to-remove pin feathers, so bare hands it was.

After the chickens were defeathered, the women grabbed them, and over flames singed off the remaining pin feathers creating an acrid smell of burning flesh and plumage. Then my brother and I removed any remaining pin feathers with our fingernails one at a time from the warm bodies.

On the table each chicken butt was sliced open revealing a glistening tangle of dark intestines bulging blue and black. The workers thrust their hand inside, grabbed the guts, and pulled them out with a giant sucking sound: sluuuurrrp!

While they worked, Grandma Fetzer talked about all the hard work she had done butchering chickens every year since she was a little girl. At some point Grandpa Fetzer chimed in, sputtering to her in German, probably about religion, as I heard him saying *Kottich*, or church, and she replying *Bupteest,* or Baptist, and quoting Bible verses in English for the benefit of us all.

117

She waved her knife in the air, swishing it around the grass, and spoke of how God was everywhere. My mouth dropped open. Everywhere? In the gaping chicken mouths? In their spraying blood? In their hearts, livers, and gizzards? In their blue intestines? In their butt-holes? In their poop? I shook my head. Couldn't be.

While I worried about being struck across the side of the head by her waving knife, she had a discussion with Grandpa. I didn't understand most of it, but it was heated, his in German, hers half and half English and German. Their differences were exacerbated by their flashing knives as they chopped the feet and legs off. So I stayed clear.

Hearts, livers, and gizzards were piled on the table, delicacies for delicious meals for the next few days, as well as necks, legs, and feet. Almost every part of the chicken was used.

The remains were cut into parts, thighs and breasts and drumsticks packed in quart-sized Ball jars to be canned and stored in the cool basement for winter.

In a few short hours, after we cleaned up, we were all deeply satisfied. The adults for the meals and me that chicken guard duty was done for a year. Freedom once more.

My First Paying Job

The summer I turned nine I was playing with my slingshot in the alley half a block away from home, looking for sparrows to shoot.

"You!" A woman yelled from her open screen door, looking at me. "Come over here!"

Uh-oh, I thought, first Mrs. Boettcher, my neighbor up the street always watching me, and now this gray-haired lady. Was I never to have peace?

I hid my slingshot behind my buttock, and dropped it behind a convenient patch of large-leaved rhubarb plants as I walked onto her lawn. Maybe she hadn't seen me drop it, and I could convince her I didn't have one, for surely my sudden troubles had to be about the slingshot.

"Can't you walk any faster?" She said, shading her eyes with a hand. As I neared she muttered in a low voice, "Maybe I made a mistake. Well, nothing for it now."

I had no idea what she was talking about.

She looked me up and down. "You're strong enough to push a lawnmower?"

I nodded.

"Okay. You'll do. Follow me."

I shrugged, and followed, suddenly realizing I'd unknowingly been auditioning for a job. Which I did not want. I just wanted to be free.

"My husband died," she said, wiping her eyes, "and I don't have anyone to cut my lawn."

She showed me how to wield her reel mower. She pushed and grunted, the blades whirred, and green snippets of grass flew into the catch-basket in back.

"Now, young man," she said, dabbing her forehead with a handkerchief, "I am Mrs. Grant and I want you to cut my entire lawn." She swept her arm across the great green expanse. "Front and back. In exchange I will reward you the munificent sum of fifty cents per hour."

I didn't know what munificent meant, but I did know about fifty cents. Fifty cents an hour! In my mind's eye I envisioned the riches piling up high into the sky. My interest suddenly skyrocketed.

I grasped the lawn mower handles, and just as Mrs. Grant turned back towards her house, I asked her what time it was. She frowned as she glanced at her wrist. "It's 1:30, young man. You're on my dime, so get hopping."

I pushed the lawn mower up and down her lawn what seemed like dozens of times, then knocked on her door. "Water?" I asked. She frowned again, and disappeared. I peered into the darkness of the house until I located a wall clock. 1:45. A quarter of an hour. Almost 15 cents already! I gulped the water, and returned to the lawn mower.

More trips up and down the long lawn and I rapped her door again. She looked annoyed. "What time is it now?"

"Goodness sakes, she said. It's 1:55. Back to work now. You're burning daylight."

She clicked the door shut, while I calculated my riches. Almost 20 cents!

The sun burned my neck as I forced the mower up and down the lawn even more times. An eternity later, I knocked again. "What now?" she said peevishly, peering past my shoulder. "Is that all you've cut so far?"

"I don't have a watch," I said. "So I can't figure out how much I've earned so far."

She frowned yet again and her face grew dark. "Young man, if that's all you can think about, then..."

She pursed her lips. "Wait here." Buoyed, I figured she was going to grab me a nice cold ice cream bar or Popsicle. "Orange," I wanted to say.

Instead a minute later she pressed a quarter into my palm. She pointed over my shoulder. "You're fired," she said. "Begone." She slammed the door.

Thus ended my first paid job, and I couldn't have been happier. I retrieved my slingshot, stuck it in my back pocket, and headed three blocks up town for a Dairy Queen.

The Watchers

After walking home from school one spring day in sixth grade, and stepping into our house, I saw Mom on the telephone. She looked at me and said, "I'll ask him."

She held her hand over the mouthpiece, and said, "Mrs. Boettcher..."

Seemed like Mrs. Boettcher saw everything that occurred in our neighborhood. Maybe she possessed a one-way window with a telescope to observe and record all the goings-on in our street in secret.

A sense of foreboding washed over me. What kind of work did Mrs. Boettcher want me to do? Or what had I done wrong now? She wouldn't call Mom to say how good one of Alma's little boys had been.

Mom said, "She wants to know why you always walk with your head down."

I frowned. As I walked, I examined at everything: cars at Aipperspach's Gas Station kitty-corner from the elementary school, sparrows in the trees, cracks in the sidewalk, rock walls lining the walks in front of the houses, *marravarich* in the empty lot, grain elevators stretching up high towards God in the great blue sky.

And I studied the ground and grass and macadam. I didn't want to miss anything. Gifts to my seeking mind.

To know that I was being studied day after day ("Why does he always...") chilled me. I passed her house twice a day going to and from school. Did I need to take another route? I shivered.

I already felt over-watched by my folks, Grandma Fetzer, teachers, church people, and the town in general. It seemed their life goals were to catch me doing wrong. This all interfered with my clarion cry of freedom to do what I desired.

To answer Mom, I shrugged. Seemed obvious. "To find money."

A few weeks earlier, because I was looking down, I spotted a fluttering five-dollar bill, caught on a *marravarich* plant near the empty lot. My heart bumped when I thought of it. Five dollars was a lot of money. More often I found a penny here or nickel there. Once an old quarter in the garden!

Mom told Mrs. Boettcher what I'd said. Then she said "Uh huh, I'll tell him," and hung up.

"Mrs. Boettcher says if you're not careful your neck is going to grow that way and you'll get humpbacked like Zelda Kraken. She says walking like that is not good for your posture."

"But it's good for finding money."

Regardless of Mrs. Boettcher's certainty, I continued to search for coins. And other items more valuable than money that turned up: agates and colored rocks, Popsicle sticks to make little rafts, brittle leaves, ants scurrying with seeds or dead prey, or locked in mortal combat, a thousand things, like money, that interested me.

But after that phone call, each time as I neared the Boettcher house, I kept my head up, though I turned my eyes down and still scanned the ground farther ahead of me, looking for exciting things, until I was safely past.

Summer Fair

When I was twelve, my friend Tom and brother Ron and I decided to become entrepreneurs, Barnums and Baileys of the Great Plains, creating a fair, loosely modeled on the Tri-County Fair held a mile west of town each August.

On a couple of telephone poles we stapled crudely-made posters screaming "Summer Fair," but most of our advertising came through word of mouth.

Fair attendees paid a nickel to enter, and discover Madame Future's Mysterious Curtained Booth, Rocks Fresh from the Moon, Boozer the Trained Cat, and the Amazing Mouse Maze. We also had a magnifying glass to examine insects in jars – close-ups of bumblebees, grasshoppers, mosquitoes, lightning bugs, and others, crawling on the inside of the jar, or flying, or upside down on the bottom, legs thrust up, dead. We wanted cockroaches too, but nobody had the courage to ask the kids who we thought lived with them to produce a few of the ugly little beasts.

Our fair was held in the corner behind Tom Klein's L-shaped house, where we were shielded from the hot summer sun. The shade protected our delicate menagerie of small furry mice and gophers and insects from expiring, and filling the air with indescribable odors. Not good for business.

Step right up! Here's Madame Future, to predict your life! But Madame Future was not our biggest money-maker, as I'd thought she would be. Even she could not have predicted that it would be the Nickel Roll.

In the Nickel Roll customers rolled a five-cent piece down a slot onto a large piece of cardboard divided by black crayon into various-sized squares, each with a number from one to ten. Any nickel that stopped entirely inside a square won that number of nickels. Any that touched a black line became house property.

Snakes were profitable too. We captured them from under bales in the fields near town. Fair-goers could view and

123

handle garter or racer snakes. Neither was poisonous or slimy as some people feared, unless the legless reptiles of Bible-fame peed on one's hands out of excitement. I hoped one fat garter snake would produce babies. What an attraction that would be! But she died after the first day. Our other animal attractions included the Frog Pond with live frogs and toads to handle.

Slingshot Shot proved successful for everyone else except the house, as we hadn't taken into account that every kid in town was proficient with a slingshot. So we lost a lot of cash before we closed that game.

The fair lasted only two days, due to the frequent shuffling off this mortal coil of our bees, mosquitoes, and fireflies. Snakes and furry mammals escaped overnight from our poorly-made cages, many of cardboard, or died, which meant messy and stinky cleanup. Which meant restocking. But who would run the fair while we hunted for replacements?

We also got bored. Summer offered many other excitements – catching minnows, playing baseball, cowboys and Indians, and so on. So we closed down with a profit of about $3 each, having learned a few lessons, too.

Playing at War

Reminders of war surrounded me everywhere,
starting with my father's bullets in Mom's sewing kit.

Uncle Howard Delzer's war booty was hidden in the
open rafters in the basement of our house. They arrived after
Howard had another war nightmare, waking in the middle of
the night in bed with his hands squeezing his wife Minnie's
neck. He thought removing his war mementos from his
house might prevent the nightmares.

So our rafters held the Arisaka bolt-action rifle he had
liberated from the body of a Japanese soldier he had killed in
hand-to-hand combat. A bayonet with the rifle didn't fit, so I
taped it to the barrel and played like I was fighting an enemy
face-to-face, imagining Howard's battle.

Other items included bullets, thin papers with
Japanese writing, some currency, and most fascinating,
drawings of Japanese couples in varied sexual positions
printed on thin onion skin paper.

Howard's discolored canvas cot was also stored in our
basement, stained with enemy blood – so we thought –
though Howard said it was jungle rot.

When our house was packed with overnight people, I
sometimes slept on that cot, inhaling the ancient war smell.
The odor kept me awake for a while, thinking of soldiers
killing each other, and imagining my father fighting in the
war, trying to save his life. And thus mine.

Mom's photo album provided additional war
reminders of pictures of soldiers taken overseas, and after
returning home. Former servicemen around town reminded
me of war, like a trio of brothers who carried the nicknames
Hitler, Stalin (sometimes Mussolini) and Tojo, because the
face of one resembled the Japanese warlord.

The postmaster when we picked up our papers each
morning limped from a wound. A carpenter who worked on
our house wheezed due to a WW I mustard gas attack.

Another veteran lived with us for a while, a hard-drinking survivor of maiming in WWII island fighting. His face and arms were twisted and disfigured. Often he lay on the couch in our living room, a lit cigarette between his yellowed fingers. The wood floor was dotted with black burnt splotches where he had fallen asleep or passed out and dropped a burning cigarette.

We lived amidst veterans from three wars, and all those reminders of war made our playing games with weapons and killing each other seem normal and natural.

Another war casualty lived up the hill on the far side of the group of trees next to Grandma and Grandpa Fetzer's. Sometimes in the dark night when the world was too much with him, and I was outside, I heard the screen door of his house slap as he stepped out.

After a short pause, he played "*Taps*" on his bugle, the pain of losing his fallen comrades cascading out through those notes. They rose and fell, and then climbed higher and higher, to the highest pitch, which he drove out into the darkness, a clear ringing note of such heart-rending pain, high, pure, and long, ten seconds, twenty, as though to reassure his long-dead fellow soldiers that he had not forgotten them. Sometimes he played "Reveille" over and over again as though attempting to wake the compatriots he had lost in World War I.

Perhaps then he found some peace.

Smoke and Fire

While gutter crawling on Main Street one summer afternoon when I was twelve, I picked up a butt and cried triumphantly, "This one has lipstick on it!" The acme of used cigarettes! Smoked by a woman! My partners in crime, Ron and Tom, admired it, too.

Each of us clutched Popsicle sticks to throw adults off the scent of our real enterprise: poking the debris for cigarette butts with half an inch or more of tobacco left.

When an adult drifted near, obviously curious about why we were on all fours in the gutter in front of the stores, we short-circuited any questions they could ask as we held up a Popsicle stick and yelled, "Look! Another one!"

They smiled indulgently and shook their heads and went on their way.

Many adults I knew except Mom and Grandma Fetzer regularly puffed clouds of smoke out of their lips, so my desire to smoke seemed normal. Even manly.

Though Walter smoked, cigarettes didn't grab my interest until I spotted a smoldering butt one morning outside the post office. I grabbed it, stuck it in my lips, inhaled, and coughed out a stream of white smoke. My brother Bob laughed. I was cool!

So Tom and I decided to take up smoking. Because Tom's dad smoked Marlboros, and Walter smoked Old Gold, we had what we thought was an inexhaustible source. We each stole a pack.

After school we pedaled our bikes furiously down to the old boxcars near the grain elevators. Six faded old red railroad cars with grain stored inside surrounded a cozy plaza of sand where nobody came, and nobody could see us.

We goofed around, smoking two-fingered like in the movies, or two cigarettes at once, or squeezed between our lips while inhaling and choking, or clenched in our teeth. We puffed away, croaking and laughing maniacally. We were cool!

We dug a hole in the sand in the middle of the plaza to hide our cigarettes. But soon we smoked them all. I was ready to liberate another pack from Walter until one night after supper he shook his open carton of Old Golds several times toward his palm. When nothing dropped out, he peered inside and frowned. "I could have sworn I had one more pack left." He gazed hard at me.

Tom couldn't steal more from his father, either. Too dangerous. I remembered smoking that butt that I found in front of the Post Office, so we figured we could find more used butts in the uptown gutters.

But few were still smokeable, either crushed, short, dirty, or gross with saliva. After raking through the gutters and finding all the useable smokes, we had to wait at least a week for people to throw away enough for us to find.

So during lean times we broke off long dried weeds from the empty lot. They flamed easily, and burned down quickly, scorching our fingers. Worse, the acrid smoke stung our lungs, and we suffered severe coughing jags.

Uncool. Set me thinking. What was the big deal? Why was I smoking? I didn't get it. I lost interest.

After that Tom and his brother Ron made corncob pipes, using "tobacco" from the shavings from my pencil sharpener. But that ended too. Our smoking experiment was tossed onto the ash-heap of history.

The baseball rebounding porch, the turret, and a piece of our house.

Walth's Turret

The six-sided turret stood at the far side of the Walth's wide cement porch running along the front of the house. The overhang was held up by four large pillars, which made the porch look like an ancient Roman temple, and the house doubly exotic.

Three windows ran up each of the six sides. Six slanted roofs met at a pipe at the summit above the top of the house. Had the turret been built separately and pressed into the corner, or erected with the original house? I was consumed with curiosity. What was inside?

One summer afternoon I decided the only way I would ever see the inside of the turret on our neighbor's house was to sneak inside. From delivering newspapers, I knew no other house in town possessed a turret. This more than intrigued me. I had to slip inside. Had to! But how?

We never socialized with the Walths as they weren't relatives, despite a mere ten feet separating our houses.

129

Mom wouldn't help me get inside either. "Ach," she said, "Don't be so silly."

Nor could I knock on Walth's door and ask to see the round rooms. A kid just didn't do something like that. Thus I was left with one option: sneaking in to examine the turret when they were gone.

"It's not a turret," my high-school-aged cousin Mylo said, perching on the rock wall in our front yard from where we could see part of the turret. "It's a silo, just like on farms."

I frowned. With Mylo you never knew what to believe. "Mom said it was a turret, with round rooms."

"Round rooms? Why would anyone want round rooms in their house? What good would they be? Everything put in a room is square – chairs, beds, dressers, everything! Think, Billy, Nothing would fit. So it's a silo. They fill it with corn for the animals in the shed back there."

"What animals? I've never seen any back there." I would have seen them or heard them when my brother and I played ball thirty feet from that shed. Or certainly when I leaped over Mrs. Walth's narrow garden strip between our houses to grab an errant baseball or wiffle ball near the shed and bring it back.

"Well," Mylo said, "they don't have animals always."

I frowned again. "Then why does the turret…"

"Silo," he interrupted.

"…have windows? Look." I pointed.

Mylo glanced at the turret and seemed surprised at my question about the windows. "Oh, well, I, um, maybe the windows tell them how much corn is left inside."

"Well, why don't farm silos have windows then?"

"Some of them do," he said. "I've seen them."

"I've never seen any."

"Well, I have." Which ended that.

So how could I accomplish my goal? First, Walths had to be gone, the house empty. Second, Mom couldn't see me. And third, my watchers across the street, Grandma Fetzer and Mrs. Boettcher, had to be inside or gone, or they would report me to Mom. Boom! Billy in trouble again. I'd have to be vigilant to have all three occur at the same time.

A few days later, I was in our back yard smacking rocks with a bat into the empty lot across the street when the Walths walked out. He inserted a key and locked the door. The back door. I didn't think anybody in town locked their doors. We certainly didn't.

But he was different. He was a grouch. If our baseball or basketball or wiffle ball drifted over into his yard while we were playing and he was outside, he held it hostage for a few days. Usually the stolen item appeared in our backyard a couple of days later. But still.

He didn't disappoint me. He studied me swinging the bat for a few seconds and shook his head in disgust. "All you ever do is play?" he said. I ignored him and kept swinging.

They got in their car and drove away. If only he hadn't locked the door! I grumped. He'd just blown my chance to get in and see the turret.

"Damn," I said. I threw up a rock and whacked it onto their siding, making a small dent. Oops! I frowned. Served the grouch right.

Then I remembered the turret windows. The Walths were gone. Nobody else lived in the house, so I smiled. Maybe I could get a peek into one round room. Better than nothing.

I hustled along the back of their house until I saw the turret at the front. All the windows were shrouded with yellowish shades and white curtains along the edges.

Would any cracks in the curtains allow me to peer in? As I stepped toward the turret, I spotted Grandma Fetzer outside. "Darn!" I muttered again. I turned back and jumped across Walth's garden into our backyard, threw down the bat and rocks, and headed to the front of our house.

I walked on the sidewalk past Walths. My plan B was to examine the other turret windows for a possible peek-in opening, without looking suspicious. So I went up the hill to our garden, and back, studying the turret windows each way.

They were all closed and covered. Except one! The highest one on the south side. Halfway open, shade up, a breeze fluttering the white curtains. Of course! Cool air!

I smacked my fist into my palm. A break! On hot summer days Mom opened and closed various windows, for better airflow. Most mothers in town did. As did Mrs. Walth.

That high open window did me no good. I'd need a ladder, a dead giveaway to anyone who saw me. But Mrs. Walth probably opened low windows at different times, windows I could peer into! Maybe even climb through into the turret! I shivered thinking of it.

My joy was tempered by two days of cool weather and rain. No open windows in town, including Walth's.

Finally, a clear day allowed the beating sun to torture me while I hoed potatoes in the morning. But after lunch, with the buzz of cicadas increasing as the temperature soared, accompanied by chirps of crickets accelerating in the rising heat, I saw Mom had opened several of our windows. Mrs. Walth must have, too. The time had come. If the right one was open... My eyes grew as wide as baseballs.

I sat in the shade on the cool steps of our porch nearest the Walth house reading a science fiction book, alternating my attention between watching Walths' front door, and listening for the sound of their car in the back yard. Many pages later a car pulled up in front of Walth's, and surprise! Mr. Walth got out and entered the house.

How had I missed hearing the car start in the back yard? Maybe too engrossed in my book. Or he left earlier.

Minutes later, the Walths walked out and down into their car. I sat up straight. They hadn't locked the door!

My heart raced. I took a deep breath to stop from jumping up and running down our sidewalk and up on their porch, guilt painted all over me. I looked at Grandma Fetzer's. Nobody out, nor at Boettcher's either. Too hot.

Now doubts surfaced. This was real. I was afraid. What if things went wrong? What if I got caught? Would they call the cops? Would I end up in jail? I gulped.

I'd never broken into a house before. But I wasn't really breaking in, I told myself, because I wasn't going to bust down the door or destroy anything inside or steal anything. I just wanted to look at those round rooms.

I tried to spit. My mouth was dry. If Mom caught me... My heart pounded. Nearly changed my mind. Walth's car disappeared over the hill. Now or never!

I needed to act innocent in case my watchers were peering out. So I stood on the wall in front of our house as I had many times before, my arms outthrust, and walked on it. With mincing steps I sidled onto the connecting stone wall in front of Walths, teetering past their front lawn, and onto their lower steps. Then I walked to the front door. I wanted to glance around again, but feared looking guilty.

Nonchalantly I climbed the steps onto their porch and pulled open the screen door, which groaned as loud as the roar of a lion. But victory was at hand! I'd make it quick. I grabbed the doorknob, turned it, pushed the door open, and was ready to sneak in.

But my knee thumped hard against the inner door. The doorknob hadn't turned. Cold in my palm, it resisted with a little click each time I tried to turn it. Couldn't believe my bad luck. Locked. He hadn't used his key.

How in the world? "Damn damn damn," I swore. I had taken all these chances... I stood stupefied.

Must be some way to get in. Must be! I tested the doorknob once more. No. Slowly closed the door. Looked at the turret. My God! Open window right there! Low! White curtains billowing.

My joy soared. I felt like screaming with happiness. Giddily, I rushed over, and glanced in to a round room there before me. If I could get the screen off... I reached out.

Behind me a man's harsh voice shouted. "Hey, what are you doing? Get away from there!"

I whirled. Mr. Walth raced up the steps, keys in his hand. Uh oh. Trouble. Real trouble.

"What are you doing on our porch?" He glared at me.

When Walths weren't around, or we thought they weren't, we bounced a baseball off the side of their cement porch and fielded the rebound, time and time again. My only chance.

"Oh," I lied, "I um was throwing the baseball off your porch and it missed, and it came up here..." I pointed at the turret.

His head swiveled. "What baseball? I don't see any baseball." He looked at the porch.

"Oh, I, uh, threw it real hard. Maybe it bounced into Wagner's yard." I waved my hand. "I'll go check."

He shook his head slowly, glaring at me. The breeze blew gently against my sweaty forehead, wafting the smell of flowers. His keys jingled, "How many times do I have to tell you boys not to throw baseballs off my porch? I told your parents. It ruins the paint and chips the cement. It costs money to fix. I have half a mind to call the cops."

He must have seen the terror in my eyes because he said, "I will, too, unless you promise never to throw a baseball off my porch again. Promise?"

My heart racing, I nodded, and promised. Which I kept. No baseballs off the porch. Nor did I ever attempt to see more of the round rooms in the turret. I had to be satisfied with that one short glimpse.

The Scharf Blacksmith Shop

Martian Blacksmith

A white building with a high cement front stood a block away from our house near the town water tower. In black letters above the door the sign said Scharf Blacksmith Shop, a place of supreme mystery to a nine-year-old like me.

Often bright rays of silver light shot out of the black square of the door, half-blinding me as though attempting to prevent me from seeing inside. As soon as I glanced away, out of the corner of my eye I noticed that the rays stopped. When I gazed back they began anew, and I had to turn away. Something mysterious was afoot. Must be an alien!

One day when I was in the back yard playing badminton with Ron, I heard the bzzzt and sizzle of the rays. Maybe the alien was attempting to repair his spaceship so he could zoom back up into the stars?

The creature wielding the ray gun was clever. Whenever I played in the nearby pigweed forest, or floated on a raft in the pond across the street from the shop, the alien spotted me. Instantly he altered his spaceship work to look as though he was repairing a plow or disc or other farm-related implement. I was amazed at his magical instant switch.

One day as I walked to my friend Tom's house next to the blacksmith shop, the alien stepped out and began working. A thrill trickled down my spine. Looking at him, I knew my suspicions were correct. He was dressed otherworldly, swathed in heavy dark clothes with a large helmet and elbow-length gloves so not a stitch of his green skin showed. Maybe he'd been sent from Mars to Earth to figure out how to take us over!

His huge helmet sported a dark visor in front, and covered his head entirely and allowed him to breathe Martian air in our atmosphere. He gripped a ray gun in his right hand. I forgot about Tom, and realized I was too close to the alien. Time for me to fly! Suddenly he flipped up the visor, and looked right at me! Yeep! I was dead!

Then a most astonishing thing happened. Just as I turned to run, he called my name. Could he read minds? This was serious!

"You're Billy, aren't you," he said. I couldn't take a step. My muscles wouldn't work. "I'll pay you to pick up these used welding rods I've thrown all over the place here," he said, indicating the ground in front of his shop with a gloved hand. Short gray metallic rods half as thick as a pencil were strewn all over. I'd heard about welding from my farm cousins but had never seen it in action.

I raised my eyes and was shocked to see that his face was pink just like mine. Even more shocking, I recognized him!

He attended our church. Not a Martian? Couldn't be sure. Maybe he'd assumed the identity of the man in church. Should I ask him? But if he thought I knew, I could be in danger! So I kept quiet.

He held out an empty gallon pail. Just then Tom came out of his house and said, "Hi, Mr. Scharf."

I told Tom he wanted me to pick up old welding rods.

"Okay," Tom said. "Knock when you're done."

So I began to pick up the one-or two-inch remnants of welding rods, marveling that I was working for someone who might be a Martian, I kept an eye on him. Couldn't be too sure.

Mr. Scharf lowered his helmet, raised it again. "Don't watch. I'm welding a broken plow share. The light can permanently damage your vision. Even blind you. That's why I wear this dark visor."

He pulled it down again and began to work with his ray gun, which he said was a welding gun, which crackled and sizzled, fixing broken metal pieces by welding them together.

When he was finished, with one hand he lifted an end of the plow and rolled the implement away from the front door, set it down next to the building, and stepped inside. I was amazed – it took strength to do that. I grabbed the plow and attempted to move it, but it didn't budge. Maybe he was a Martian!

I was intrigued. I'd never been inside a blacksmith shop. I picked up more rods and dropped them clicking into the pail. Then my curiosity got the best of me. I carried the pail to the black door, and peered in.

He was working by a forge fire, using long tongs to grip a chunk of metal he held in the orange flames. I watched in delight as the piece grew orange, then crimson. He pulled it out of the fire and clunked it on a huge anvil set on a block of wood, that made a comfortable working height for him. A heavy burnt smell permeated the air. He easily picked up a great hammer, large and heavy as an Indian war club, and smacked the red-hot chunk of metal. He was strong. Maybe all Martians were. I smiled.

Orange sparks sprayed after every clamorous clang, clang, clang, of the blows. The sounds raced out the door and rang against the great metal granary half a block away, and echoed against the grain elevators nearby. After more pounding and examining, he plunged the dimming-red metal hissing into a dark tub of what looked like oil. The air filled with more unfamiliar burning smells.

Enthralled, I stepped inside. The shop was filled with unfamiliar tools, machines with pulleys and belts, a gasoline engine in a corner, walls covered with strange objects hanging on nails: old horseshoes, large shears, bent rods. A long workbench ran along one wall with a few scattered tools, with others hanging on nails on the wall behind it.

When he saw me, he said, "Done out there?"

Before I could answer, he removed his gloves and dug a couple of quarters out of his pocket, handed them to me, and took the pail.

Over the years I helped pick up his cast-off debris several more times, because his shop was unusual, and either a Martian or an Ed Scharf was equally exciting, and I liked him.

Stealing Chokecherries

Elizabeth was Grandpa Woehl's second wife, after his first died.

We thrived on homemade chokecherry jelly, but without chokecherry trees in our yard, we had to procure the fruit elsewhere. One year Mom said the berries in Grandpa Woehl's backyard were ripe, so we should go pick them. We carted a ladder and empty Karo syrup pails four blocks to their place and turned into their alley. Their trees groaned with the black fruit.

I climbed the ladder for high berries. Bob and Ron picked low ones. I grabbed plump handfuls and stripped black berries off, clattering them into my pail. Smiling, I licked the juice off my wet palms, and every fifth clump I ate, reveling in the sweet tart taste, spitting the BB-sized pits onto the ground, and reaching for more. Their smell was in the air.

My pail was half full when I heard the screen door of their house open. Grandpa and Grandma Woehl rushed out, yelling, "*Vass dusht du?*" (What are you doing?)

They hurried toward us, speaking angrily in German. I understood *stehlen* (stealing.) I was scared and wanted to run. With juice still dripping down my chin and a mouthful of berries bulging my cheeks, I was the poster child for stealing their chokecherries.

Bob said, "Mom said we could pick them."

"*Vass?*" (What?) Grandpa said.

"We're Alma's boys," Bob said.

"*Vass? Ich denksht nit,*" (What? I think not,) Grandpa said. "*Du bischt zu gross!*" (You are too big.) He accused us of stealing, so we grabbed the ladder and fled.

139

School Tightrope

Creating Abraham Lincoln

I attended this grade school for six years.

At birth, I was gifted with a wild untamed beast of imagination. As I grew older, I created make-believe worlds to crawl inside, and populate with imaginary characters, actions and stories.

My red-hot imagination was often laid across the anvil of conformity and pounded out of shape by the hammer of negativity.

The classroom proved to be a great enemy of my imagination. Our fourth-grade teacher handed out black construction paper, and said to create Abe Lincoln's profile, like on the bulletin board. I grabbed my scissors.

"No," she said, knocking them out of my hands. "With your fingers. Tear it like this. Use your imagination."

I gasped, excited for the official sanction to use the part of my brain that always fired on eight cylinders.

I tore out Abe's eye indentation, ripped off pieces of construction paper to form his nose, lips, chin, and beard.

Though the example on the board didn't show hair, I made some. He did have hair, after all. The result was a lumpy top and back of his head. When I held it at arm's distance, the bust kind of looked like Abe.

I smiled and raised my hand and proudly showed it to our teacher. She snapped it out of my grasp and said, "What's this?"

"Abraham Lincoln," I said.

"It most certainly is not. Try again," she said, tossing it back on my desk, handing me another sheet of black construction paper. "Look at the board."

That day I learned that to some people "Use your imagination" didn't mean giving my wild-eyed beast free rein. Rather it meant, "Do it like I did it."

The constant knife cuts of criticism dribbled the lifeblood out of my imagination at school. But despite the slings and arrows flung at my imagination during elementary and middle school, it persisted because it was born large and strong in me and strengthened because Mom read to us when we were young. I snuggled up against her warm side and sighed, listening with rapt wonder to every word from *The Big Book of Fairy Tales.* I could imagine how beautiful the beauty was in *Beauty and the Beast,* and the awful beast. I saw the genie pop out of the bottle to offer wishes. I heard the Giant cry, *"Fee-fi-fo-fum! I smell the blood of an Englishman. Be he alive, or be he dead, I'll grind his bones to make my bread.*

Wow! I didn't know that's how bread was made.

But I was more thrilled with these stories and others Mom chose which allowed my imagination to run amok, forming wondrous scenes in response to the words that poured from her mouth.

More important, Mom didn't criticize my imaginative outpourings: how did Rapunzel wash her hair? Or how did spinning wheels make gold? She let me believe what I wanted. Mom's unintentional support of my flights of fancy can't be weighted or calibrated. It balanced what was taken from me.

Hazards of Beauty

Our new fourth-grade teacher was a beauty – tall, slim, golden-haired – and I fell in love with her before the end of the first day.

At recess I hung back shyly on the playground while a gaggle of excited kids surrounded her. I sidled next to her and studied the long slender fingers of her hand, as a parched desert traveler eyes a water-filled oasis. I was enveloped by perfume and closed my eyes in ecstasy.

In Looney-Tune cartoons characters are sometimes lifted up off the ground and drawn sinuously through the air by a scent come alive. That's exactly how I felt standing next to her and her heady perfume, brought to life, elevated, uplifted into a better plane. I slipped my hand into hers.

She leaped as though I'd stuck a hot branding iron into her palm. "Don't do that, little boy," she hissed, jerking her hand away and hiding it behind her. I backed away, my mouth open, and fled to the far end of the playground.

She had decorated our classroom with dark green wall charts showing cursive writing, others to record student tooth-brushing, large red and orange construction paper tree leaves, fine-looking like her enthralling beauty.

Except for the old dusty curtains on the six-foot-high windows. For the first month it seemed like every time I glanced up at her she was gazing at them, tapping her chin.

Until one morning when we stepped into our classroom to see a stunning white shimmer of lacy curtains on all the windows. "I made them," she said proudly. "Aren't they lovely?" And they were.

By then I'd realized my gorgeous-on-the-outside teacher was not nearly so beautiful on the inside. She seemed to enjoy pinching the backs of arms or yanking the hair of boys who didn't spell well, or whispered, or were rowdy.

At first, perhaps the admiration in my eyes exempted me, or that I was a good, silent, trouble-free student.

Contraband Chocolate Milk

Each Friday the Wishek Creamery deposited half-gallons of chocolate milk in the entryway to the school. Each time our teacher sneaked down early and liberated one or two extra half-gallons of the prized brown milk, shorting other classes. She hid the stolen merchandise in the wastebasket beside her desk, and covered it with papers.

After our regular half-gallons had been emptied, she reached into the wastebasket and lifted out the first additional half-gallon of chocolate milk. "This is a bonus just for you, girls and boys," she said, smiling. "A special present from me." She clattered up and down the rows in her high heels, filling our cups.

If we said we didn't want more, she snatched our cup, filled it, and smacked it back down on our desk, splashing chocolate milk around. "I got this milk for you," she said menacingly. "Now drink it."

Which we did.

And got sick. Some kids threw up. While soaking up another mess with sawdust, the janitor asked our teacher why so many of her students threw up Fridays. After that, we had to clean up our own messes.

One Friday the principal, Mrs. Graham, knocked, and stepped in. Sighing, she asked our teacher if she might have accidentally picked up two extra half-gallons of chocolate milk, as two were missing again this week.

"Why, no," she said sweetly. "You may check if you like." She swept her ballerina arm gracefully across the room.

"Liar, liar, pants on fire," I wanted to yell, "*Mrs. Graham, she's lying. Look in the wastepaper basket. Under all the paper.*"

But I was scared, and said nothing.

Nor did anyone else. Cowed, we sat, hands in our laps, feet flat on the floor, eyes staring straight ahead, terrified that Mrs. Graham might ask one of us about the milk, and bring our teacher's judgment crashing down on our heads, making our lives even more miserable.

Yet my hope of love remained blind. As Halloween neared, I decided to impress our teacher with the most perfect jack-o'-lantern ever made. She would smile when she spotted my gift to her. Maybe she would adore me. Maybe she would become sweet, like the princesses Mom had read about. Maybe.

The afternoon of the party a dozen jack-o-lanterns rested on the wide window ledge with candlelight flickering cheerily through cut-out eyes and noses and jagged mouths. I waited expectantly for her surprised reaction to my large jack-o'-lantern. But the day wore on, and the praise never came.

Disappointed, I was bobbing for apples when David screamed "Fire!" Everyone whirled and saw an orange tongue of flame licking at two curtains, crawling towards the ceiling, billowing acrid smoke.

David snatched a blazing jack-o'-lantern and screeched, "Billy's pumpkin is burning your curtains!"

Someone opened the window and he flung the flaming pumpkin out in a beautiful streaming arc of color. The orb shattered into orange and black smoldering fragments on the snow-white playground two stories below.

I glanced at my teacher. Her eyes were fixed on me, icy and glittering. She could just as well have whispered in my ear, "Little boy, you will pay."

A couple of days later she appeared at our house, smiling too widely. She patted my head, and sweetly told Mom what a nice, smart boy I was. I was astonished. Who was this imposter, I kept thinking? But my heart calmed. Everything would be all right!

While sitting in the living room they drank coffee and chatted and laughed like old friends, agreeing that in reparation Mom would sew new lacy gauze curtains for our room.

But back at school I was marked. Every chance the teacher could, she pinched me. If I yelled "Ow," she yanked my hair. Or slapped my arm or back with the flat of a ruler. My lips trembled as she gaily administered her little wasps of pleasure. I learned to endure them soundlessly.

I had always loved school, but I was never so glad as when the year ended.

The next year was heaven in Miss Smiley's fifth-grade classroom. We warned her about the stolen milk, so one Friday when we were shorted, she sent me back to that fourth-grade room to ask if that same teacher had taken extra chocolate milk by mistake.

I trembled as I shuffled towards the fourth-grade door. I knocked and stammered my question.

"Of course not," She said. "Why does everybody always blame me?" She jerked me in and pushed me in front of the class, grabbing a hunk of skin on my back. She pinched and twisted it, and pointed at the curtains. "This little boy tried to burn down your school building last year."

Somehow I escaped back to Miss Smiley's room before I burst into tears. When she saw my stricken face, she led me back to my desk with an arm around my shoulder. "I shouldn't have sent you. I should have gone myself."

Each time afterwards when I saw my fourth-grade teacher I avoided her, but couldn't avoid reliving feeling those nails biting into my back.

Full Circle

Who would have thought playing marbles at school would devolve into trouble? But Trouble smiled, gleefully watching unworldly fifth-graders prepare themselves to get nabbed.

The size of our marble circles varied, scratched with a finger in the brown playground dirt. We dropped marbles inside, knelt, and shot to knock someone else's out of the ring, and pocket them. Good players earned four or five turns in a row. Not me; maybe two.

One morning on the playground my friends dropped marbles into the ring, but instead of kneeling, marched five steps away, and scraped a line with a heel. I was confused until I saw the dinner-plated-sized hole two inches deep teeming with marbles. Potsies, they called the new game. Loft your shooter into the pot, knock some marbles out, and keep them.

I took my turn, using my big shooter. But it had no weight like their steel shooters, dislodged no marbles, and worse, stayed in the pot. "Stays in, you lose it," someone shrugged. "That's the rule."

So I had to watch for a few days as I searched for a bigger shooter. No luck.

In desperation I agreed to buy a big steel farm machine bearing from a classmate for a dollar. A fortune. Which I didn't have. And only one way to get it.

One morning I waited until my stepdad closed the door to the bathroom, and while mom cooked breakfast, I sneaked into their bedroom. More than a dollar's worth of change lay on the bureau. I reached for it, but pulled back. No, he'd miss the change right away. But his wallet was there!

Looked like nothing but fives inside! Disaster! He'd notice if I stole a five and later replaced four ones. I panicked, cocking my ears to the sound of a door opening, or Mom's steps. Riffling the currency once more, I spied a dollar. Saved! I grabbed it just as the toilet flushed and I skedaddled out to breakfast. Mr. innocent.

With my new heavy steelie I my bag of marbles began to bulge, and I gained new respect in the eyes of my peers.

The first hint of trouble came when teachers threatened no more playing unless we filled the pot and tamped it down after each recess. They didn't seem to believe that we didn't fill the pot each time due to our desire to get back into our classrooms.

Then somebody got the bright idea to dig a pot in the dirt next to the side of the building. Nobody ever came there, so we'd never have to fill it. We played on. We learned the best way to knock marbles out of the pot was lobbing the heavy steelie right in the pot from a distance. But nobody was perfect, and some of the heavy shooters banged off the stucco side of the building. Each one chipped a small white piece loose, baring first a small spot, which grew and grew, until it was as large as a wastebasket opening.

One day, just as the recess-ending bell rang, the janitor brought the superintendent out and showed him the big bare spot. They glared at us like criminals standing in a guilty knot, attempting to hide our marbles behind us or in our pockets without the officials seeing. But too late.

First we received a lecture on taking care of the schoolhouse, "It's the only one we have, you know," Then they liberated us of every single marble, and dismissed us with threats of speaking to our parents.

Followed by double jeopardy. Because we got to class late, our next recess was taken away, and we had to stay after school cleaning boards and erasers.

I never played marbles at school again.

Gates of Freedom

One day in fifth grade Miss Smiley answered a knock on the door, turned and said, "Billy, there is a man here to see you."

I leapt to my feet, knocking my math book onto the floor with a clunk and sending a pencil skittering. My classmates looked at me with consternation, frowning at the noise that broke their concentration.

My heart thundered. A man! My father! Of course! Who else? Would he stay this time? My knees trembled and my hand was slick on the knob as I yanked the door open.

"Daddy!" I cried. I gazed up breathlessly, but instead of my father's dark brown eyes, into the gray eyes of a stranger. Hot tears blurred my vision.

He ignored them and introduced himself. "You're Billy Vossler?"

I nodded.

"How old are you?"

"T-ten," I said, wiping my eyes.

He looked me up and down. "Close enough," he said. "You start delivering Monday." He turned away.

"Delivering what?"

"The *Minneapolis Tribune* newspaper," he said, and walked away.

I was astounded. And angry. I picked up my math book and pencil and sat down hard in my desk, gritting my teeth. I had never asked to deliver newspapers. But our family was not a democracy. I'd never heard a peep of a discussion at home about adding another onerous hulk of work to my already-in-my-mind overburdened life of weeding, cleaning the basement, washing and drying dishes, and now this!

But I could not have been more mistaken about the route's effect on my life. Delivering newspapers freed me for two hours every day from the tyranny of adult supervision, giving me freedom where I could be simply me. To think

what I wanted to think; do what I wanted to do on the route
if it didn't hamper me, without interruption or castigation. A
great gift.

So each morning before school, anthems of joy
heralded me as I rose out of the cool dark cave of our
basement bedroom at the first rays of dawn, gobbled down a
bowl of Wheaties, and pedaled pell-mell to the post office
four blocks away to grab my newspapers.

Usually they were lying on the floor at the far end of
the hall. If not, I waited for the screech of the door. Then
Postmaster Teddy Brandt poked his head out, glaring at me,
as though I was responsible for his early rising. As if he was
bowling, he underhanded the bundle, grunting as he slung it
hissing down the corridor towards me. It would have knocked
me over if I hadn't skipped aside to let it skid past and thump
against the wall.

Though my major ambition in life was to avoid work
that I didn't want to do, delivering newspapers was pure gold
for me. Dropping the *Minneapolis Tribune* behind the screen
doors of my Germans from Russia customers every day was
not work.

In the full splendor of each new morning I slipped
into the godlike silence of the cathedral of deserted streets to
experience the ever-changing facets of nature: glorying in the
holy smells of the burgeoning bright flowers, and marveling
at the trills and flutterings of awakening sparrows and
chickadees. Or feeling the cool plops of raindrops on my
face, and watching them splash on the shining avenues, and
seeing spider webs bedecked with jewels of dew. Or smelling
the acrid bite of burning leaves, and feeling their brown
crunch beneath my bike tires. Or hearing the wild wailing
witch of a blizzard as it scratched my cheeks with icy claws,
frisking me through my clothes, and sucking out gouts of
white breath from my mouth. Or treading lonely tracks into
the virginal white blankets of snow to slip newspapers into
the doorwells of the dark houses in the silent town. Or the
upsliding radiance of the warming sun trickling the snow into

submission, creating suggestions of green that graduated into curled tree buds and shoots of verdant grass and the bath of warming air against my cheek.

Embraced by the changing comeliness of nature every day, her beauty became etched into my heart. I became bewitched by her charms. And in love with these wondrous gifts to my childhood.

Oh, those were golden days of youth, filled with breathless joy. As Dylan Thomas wrote in *Fern Hill*, *And as I was green and carefree…About the happy yard and singing…In the sun that is young once only, Time let me play and be Golden… All the sun long it was running, it was lovely, in the sun born over and over, I ran my heedless ways…*

But I did not realize that those days would not last. Those halcyon days were numbered, already in their death throes, and would pass away, never to return, not for me, nor for anyone else evermore.

Half a Building

When I was eight, I was invited to a birthday party in
the Plamor, a roller skating rink outside town owned by a
classmate's father, and my great uncle. Roller-skating sounded
exciting to others but not to me.

My classmates wheeled about the 60-foot rink,
screeches echoing off the hardwood floor as they dodged
each other, zigzagging, thin arms flailing for balance, eyes
wide and mouths gaping in glee as they thumped lightly
against a wall or skidded and fell on their rear ends. Applause
should have broken out whenever anyone made an
untrammeled circuit of the floor.

With a couple of other cowards, I hugged the wall,
flinching when the careening shapes of smoothly-skilled girls
swept by. I didn't know how to skate. They ice skated outside
in frigid weather, never my idea of a good time.

I leaned against the boards, shakily placing one
treacherous skate ahead of the other until I completed a
wobbly, but triumphant, circuit around the hardwood floor. I
noted that everybody who fell popped up laughing and
unhurt so I gained confidence. Keeping the wall a half-step
away as a crutch, I attempted longer skates, until I could make
it nearly a quarter of the way around without falling.

Eventually we undid our skates, donned our winter
wraps, and were hustled out to cars leaking white clouds from
their exhausts, and whisked home. As we drove through the
white countryside I realized I'd had fun, and wanted to skate
again.

But fate chose to thwart me. That summer the roller
skating rink was moved from the country to a hill by the
highway east of town. But not the entire building. Bizarrely,
only half.

When I spotted the remains, I felt sad, and couldn't
believe it. What could have caused two people to cut it in
half? Deep-seated animosity, for sure. But why? To insure

151

that neither man could use it without extensive and expensive repairs?

The split raised many questions: Had the halving been mutual? Or had one man out of spite sliced the building down the middle one night, then phoned the other, saying, "Come pick up your half--?"

And how did they slice it apart? Simultaneously during hours of détente? Did they climb up to opposites sides of the peak, each with a power saw, and facing each other, snarl as they started their blades singing? Did they for the briefest moment consider using the tool as a weapon before they pressed the saws down, hearing them whine through layers of wood, tarpaper, drywall, and siding?

How long did the work take? How did they decide who got which half? A coin flip? Those questions remained forever unanswered.

Once the half-building had been moved east of town, the great gaping gash remained open to the elements, a dark cavern with electrical wires drooping from the ruptured edges, fractured laths, wallboards, insulation, and siding poking out of the ends of the walls.

A bank of dirty snow accumulated at the opening, and in the spring the runoff flowed back into the darkness, pooling against the stage, a miniature lake that shrank by degrees as the days warmed, leaving concentric arcs of dirty brown shorelines. The hardwood floor lay humped and cracked.

I never heard any details about the severed building. Just more Germans from Russia silence.

Over the years the building disappeared, leaving one more question: what happened to the other half?

Seeking Refuge

Refuge On the Roof

Our chicken coop was set beneath elm and box elder trees next to the gravel alley behind our house. The building was twenty by ten, with narrow white siding and a slanting roof. In it we raised chickens, rabbits, and pigeons for food. Along with myriads of mice, which we did not choose to eat.

That roof was my refuge. I loved the solitude. I boosted myself up onto the rough wood shingles, laid back, inhaled, and felt the tonic of freedom flow through my veins. The roof concealed me, because from its highest point in the front, it slanted down towards the alley beneath tree branches thick with leaves. There I hid my sad countenance when the world was too much with me.

Sometimes I thought uneasily of Grandma Fetzer's latest sermon. Standing on our doorstep, she punched the Bible, quoting verses which reminded me that I was a wretched sinner worthless in the sight of God. I gazed up into the sky populated with dark menacing clouds.

Signs of the end times surrounded us, she said, thumping her Bible: wars, rumors of war, wickedness, and all the sinning of the people. Clear evidence of the last days.

I was highly troubled by her pronouncements. How many days were left for me to attempt to cleanse my soul to prevent me plunging straight down into the bottomless pit of hell when the end came? Out of the corner of my eye a streak of lightning illuminated the black swollen clouds and plunged down into the earth. I jumped at the crack of thunder. I vaguely smelled rain.

I didn't understand how sins worked. I knew Adam and Eve had bequeathed me a colony of sins the second I was born. Those sins were choking me, dragging me down toward hell's raging inferno, where the searing flames would scorch my tender skin over and over again through eternity while I yelled and yowled. I shuddered.

But what could I do about it? Nothing I knew of.

When my fear drove me to talk to adults, asking how to rid myself of my sins so I wouldn't burn in hell, they didn't take me seriously. Mom said, "Ach, don't be so silly." Aunt Edna said "Ach, don't worry. Just be good."

The person I should have asked, of course, was our minister, but he was too distant and forbidding, so instead I stewed and suffered.

I was jealous of my Catholic classmates who confessed their sins each Sunday, wiping their slate clean, so they could start piling up sins once more on Monday. Maybe even Sunday afternoon. Why couldn't we do that? Or why didn't we have confession to clear all our sins away? Or why couldn't I be Catholic – even if they were "the enemy."

Every Sunday's sermon reminded me that I was still an awful sinner, having another week's collection of sins poured into my personal totebag of sin without trying, even if I was sick in bed the entire time.

But I did more than mope. Enveloped in that dappled green world, spread-eagled, the stem of a leaf clamped between my teeth, I gazed up at what I could see of the glorious blue sky above.

On that roof I observed little wonders of the world, noting how the head of a sparrow jerked upward and wings downward when it chirped; that flies pushed off backwards; that wisps of white at the edges of clouds curled and moved like stray white whiskers in a breeze; that leaves pounded by a strong wind turned backwards, revealing the lighter-colored reverse side; that birds fluttering and cheeping would be fed by other birds; that an inchworm formed an upside-down U and pushed its head forward, making its slow progress – these details from different animals set my heart singing.

If at night I gazed up into a sky splashed with the white spray of stars, the gray blanket of the Milky Way, and the Big Dipper. I smiled as I reached up and felt like I could pluck down from the firmament, and clutch them in my hand, like fireflies.

Sometimes I studied the scimitar of moon while a cooling wind sprang up, chickens below made restless clucks, and the distant bark of dogs or the "Whoo whoo whoo" of an owl met my ears.

Though I was often hiding on the chicken coop roof from the pain of the world, that negativity was more than erased, and I was buoyed by the gift of beauty that surrounded me atop the roof of our chicken coop.

Wayne and his cousin Penny Waite are with swings in our back yard in front of the chicken coop. Notice the homemade basketball hoop atop the coop.

Music of the Meadows

Some mornings I awoke to the distant rapturous Music of the Meadows summoning me out into its golden atmosphere, and I knew I must obey, or spend a day in the doldrums.

Hopping out of bed and skipping breakfast to avoid Mom and her ever-present work list, and sticking a paperback in my pocket, I delivered my newspapers in a trance, giddy with possibilities. If I could pull off my subterfuge.

Finished with my route, I stopped at the Mindt V Store downtown and bought two bags of black Nibs and a Snickers bar to get me through the rest of the day. The stop meant taking a chance, because my stepdad worked at Sayler Brothers Hardware two stores down, and if he saw my bike – or me – the jig would be up. But I needed sustenance.

With my booty in my pockets I raced my bike two blocks to the pigweed forest at the corner of the empty lot, glancing behind me for pursuit, but saw none. I walked the bike into the thick growth of pigweeds a block away from our house, leaned it against a couple in the leaf-covered dimness, and turned my mental eyes toward the meadows north of town.

My goal was to walk with joy among the denizens and hearken to their songs, peepings and croakings, buzzings and chirps, quacks and caws. Even moos. But I knew that on the way the half-open doors of discovery would distract me and lure me inside to add to my store of knowledge, or simply to provide fun, with no adult to chivvy me.

Deep in the coolness of the pigweed forest I spotted a nice thick plant, straight and unmarred, perfect for a rifle for our games. The bottom was round as a silver dollar, tapering gently to the top.

With a little effort I yanked out the plant, withdrew my pocket knife, and sliced off the roots. The rest of the day was mine, so I decided to work on the rifle right then.

A few minutes later I heard the distinctive sound of my stepdad's pickup puttering down the road. At first I ignored the truck, as I supposed it would turn the corner and head toward home, perhaps searching for me. But the vehicle stopped. Perhaps thirty feet away, by the sound of the engine. Uh oh. I glanced at my bicycle. Had the sunlight glinted off the handlebars, revealing its presence – and mine? No. Couldn't be seen. I was hidden too.

Had pulling up the plant jiggled other plants, giving me away? I closed my eyes, and hoped not.

"Billy!" Walter yelled over the idling pickup. "I know you're in there. *Schteig oof!* (Wake up.) Come out. There's work to be done!"

Well, shit. That was an invitation that didn't intrigue me. I pushed myself up, then stopped. How did he know I was in here? He didn't. He was guessing. He knew this was one of my lairs and he hoped to spook me into revealing myself.

He yelled again. I didn't move. A minute later the pickup drove away, the sound of the engine fading. I decided to head out to the Meadows immediately. I laid the plant down, turned, and pushed open the leaves to step out – and jumped right back in.

Down the street, Walter was talking to Ed Scharf at the blacksmith shop. Yeep! I waited with bated breath. Finally I heard the pickup start, and move closer to me, and then stop again. "Billy! *Du bas oof!*" (You look out!)

I didn't answer, the truck started again, the sound receding as Walter returned to work; perhaps at the store, perhaps installing tile or carpets or countertops at somebody's home.

Five minutes later, I parted the reeds, glanced both ways, inhaled, and stepped out. No trace of Walter.

Down the street on the other side, Ed Scharf was welding in front of the black square of his open doorway, bending over a green grain planter. He applied the welding rod, and amid sharp buzzing, created blinding white flashes of light. Quickly I turned my eyes away, as he'd previously warned me of the dangers.

His heavy work clothes, accentuated by the helmet and protective visor drawn down over his face, made him look like the alien I'd once thought he was. As I neared, my shoes crunched the gravel on the road, and he lifted his mask and waved a gloved hand, motioning me over.

Seemed like whenever we kids ached for money, he somehow knew and hired me or one of my brothers to earn extra cash picking up the pieces of used welding rods he tossed in front of his work yard.

Damn! I didn't want to pick up his cast-aways, even if I got paid well. I didn't want to work at all. I just wanted a day of freedom.

When I got close, he smiled. I smelled the sharp odor of welding. "Your stepdad asked if I'd seen you. I said I hadn't, because all I saw was a bicycle disappearing into those weeds over there, and I didn't know who the bike belonged to." He smiled again. "Not taking the bike?"

I could hardly speak I felt so grateful. I shook my head. "I'll probably come home by Ferchos, on the other side of the pasture."

He nodded. "How old are you?"

"Eleven," I said.

He nodded again. "Sometimes I think you boys work too hard. Well, back to it." He pulled down the visor and began welding, the bright light casting shadows of the outline of the equipment he worked on against the white stucco.

Relieved, with the sizzle of welding diminishing behind me, I walked past the mud flat on the sun-baked pond across the street in the empty lot, cracked and forming lines that created a wild array of shapes. One looked like North Dakota, another a tailless *Brontosaurus*, a third a misshapen flower. I smiled. Each could have whipped up a story in my wild imagination, but I kept walking.

On each side of the road stood a grain elevator with white siding, rising high into the prairie sky. One-and-a-half-ton trucks filled with grain idled on the ramps that led up to the open doors of both elevators.

As I crossed the railroad tracks I spotted a missing spike in a tie. I knelt and stuck my finger in the hole. Cool to have a spike of my own! The rails wouldn't miss just one, I was sure.

With my jackknife I tried to pry a spike loose. No luck. Bent the blade. Tried others. All solid, each cold black head driven deep into the tie, until the elongated head clanged against the metal plate and clamped everything down tight.

I thought the weight of the monstrous Soo Line train engines and heavy railcars lumbering back and forth would have loosened a spike or two. But none that I could see. The sharp smell of creosote filled the air.

A hundred yards beyond the railroad tracks I heard the faint peeping and croaking of frogs in the marsh and the deeper ribbit of a few toads, the sounds increasing as I neared, making me smile.

Afraid as I was of water, I hesitated before stepping down the ditch toward the shallow water at the verge of the marsh amidst the music of the frogs. For a moment I closed my eyes, inhaling the smell of the marsh, my heart filled with happiness.

When I parted the cattails and reeds and fluttered my fingers through the murky water, searching for frogs, their sounds suddenly ceased like a door slamming shut. Dozens of plops reverberated from the absconding frogs. Two remained on a lily pad leaf so I could admire their dark green bodies and brown spots. Their thin front-leg fingers on both hands were splayed open and pressed on top of the pads. Their black eyes looked at me with suspicion. At some invisible signal, both leaped into the water and disappeared. But not before gladdening my heart.

Back on the road, a hundred feet farther I crossed the bridge over Beaver Creek, a stream perhaps a dozen feet wide in a few places. The day was bright, the pasture grass deep green and inviting. Near the bridge I sat on the bank of the creek. A moment later a pair of adult mallards leading three yellow and brown puffy-feathered little ones swam in a line out from beneath the bridge. Maybe I moved, as they all suddenly reversed direction.

Or heard the cry of a killdeer, which startled a fox. The bird fluttered up and raced away, thin legs pounding the earth, right wing dragging, left wing flapping uselessly. I had to chuckle. I'd been a party to that very convincing behavior a week before, and knew its end. But the fox didn't. She rushed after the killdeer. An easy meal!

The killdeer is a beautiful bird with an orange circle around its eyes, black and white stripes on its head, chest, and wings, orangish tail with a black edge when spread, and light brown legs. Its cry mimics its name, KILL-deer, KILL-deer.

The killdeer evaded the fox's jaws, darting back and forth, acting piteously vulnerable, and drawing the fox away from its nest, while the fox had to be thinking, "Yum, lunch."

Seconds later as I lay on the grass, listening to the pleasant voice of the stream, the killdeer made its escape as one had from me that other day. The bird leaped into the air and flew swiftly away, mocking the fox with a high-pitched deedeedee deedeedee, ("Ha ha! Fooled you! And my babies are safe. Ha ha!") its wounded wing miraculously healed. A ploy to save its young! The fox gazed confounded at the disappearing bird.

I put my hands behind my head, the grass tickling my ears. The chase and escape left me amazed. Wasn't nature wonderful? What a beautiful scene! With a happy ending, no less! At least for the killdeer. And me.

I closed my eyes, feeling the warm sun caress me. A few minutes later I heard a scree from on high. A hawk, its tail a reddish stain against the brilliant blue sky, labored with a wriggling garter snake in its talons. Nature's immutable law of red in tooth and claw.

My heart was filled with delight. As I rose I realized my slingshot wasn't in my back pocket any longer. A few steps backwards. I soon found it. I opened one package of Nibs and ate a few of the black licorice treats.

I walked along the stream, admiring a few yellow and white clovers, and spiky Canadian thistle with beautiful purple flowers. I pulled the stem to smell the flower and felt the thorns. Press harder, and they would draw blood!

I also saw pink prairie roses low to the ground, full of thorns too. As I smelled them, I wondered why the stems of beautiful flowers needed thorns? Protection? From what?

Hearing the distant noon siren, I and ate my melting Snickers bar and from time to time a few Nibs, listening to the holy sound of the gurgle and tinkle of the water over stones and pebbles that served as rapids in the narrow water.

I pulled out my copy of Isaac Asimov's *I, Robot*, and read about the three laws of robotics, which intrigued me: robots could not injure humans, had to obey humans, and had to protect their own existence.

After reading a chapter, I searched for distinctive stones. I examined them and stuck a few in my pocket. I skipped flat rocks up and down the stream, and saved roundish rocks for my slingshot. I wished I hadn't brought it along, as it kept falling out from my half-torn pocket.

I tried to catch minnows, but they were too fast and slipped through my fingers. No large fish appeared.

As the hours passed, I stretched out on my back on the bank, studying the puffy clouds drifting across the sky, hearing the lowing of cows in the distance, feeling the soft breeze ruffle my hair, content in solitude, the ambient noises and cries, the Music of the Meadows.

I lost track of time, daydreaming, making up stories, until I heard the pounding clangs of a train being built on the tracks a couple of blocks away near the depot, the railroad cars cracking and slamming into each other as they were moved and reconnected.

Then I heard the distant town siren declaring six o'clock. Uh oh. Now I might be in trouble. Where had the day gone? Time to hustle, and take the shortest route home.

I ran through thistle, feeling the thorns grapple with my jeans, pulling at my legs. As I neared the tracks, all my routes of escape were closed by a long line of train cars stretching as far as my eye could see in both directions.

Had to get home. Soon! Quickest was straight ahead, crawling under a train car. I had done it before.

I was out of breath at the boxcars. The gaping opening between the sets of wheels on the unmoving train cars would make it easy. I dropped to my hands and knees. My slingshot fell out. I scrabbled for it, and stuck it back in my pocket. I was between the huge steel wheels. If one shiny wheel hit me, I'd be sliced in two! I shuddered. Quickly!

I ducked my head and reached across the first rail. My palms scraped against the rough wood of a tie under the haziness beneath the car. At that instant I heard the sound of the engine, and the train cars jolted! Crash! My knees were outside the rail. My shoulders and arms inside.

I leapfrogged over the track and landed under the car as the wheels jerked to where I had been seconds ago. "Holy shit!" I muttered. This was serious.

With me underneath, the cars began to move. I tensed, ready to leap ahead, my face nearly against a wheel. I smelled grease and creosote and fear. Had to get out from under the car. Fast. Before the train picked up speed.

One set of wheels passed. I hurtled forward into the bright daylight on the other side. My right toes struck the wheel as I shot out onto the loose rocks along the tracks.

I heard a crunch. And screamed.

But felt no pain. Except scrapings on my hands and knees. I turned. My slingshot lay cut in half. I almost puked. That could've been me! Sliced in half! Lots of blood!

I got up and raced to the pigweeds, retrieved my bicycle, and rode home. I caught holy hell, but I had sated my desire for spending hours alone in nature.

And I learned from it – I never tried to crawl under a moving boxcar again, but many times after I again obeyed the wondrous cry of the Music of the Meadows.

Grandpa Fetzer

My relationship with my step-grandfather John Fetzer was unusual because he could not speak English, and I could not speak the Germans from Russia dialect, though both of us could catch a few of each others' words from time to time. Yet we enjoyed each other's company.

In my eyes he was Grandfather, not step-grand-father, because my blood grandfathers were out of reach, and he was kind, present, and patient, unlike my absent father and distant step-father, so he was my male figure to look up to, and trust.

When we ate at Grandpa and Grandma's, I loved to watch how he prayed, and how he said the German words. He sat at the table filled with food, bowed his head, clasped his hands, and leaned forward, pressing his forehead against his thumbs, mirroring the white-haired man in the painting "The Grace" also praying.

Grandpa's prayer began barely above a whisper, the same prayer each time, *"Kommen sie Herr Haysoos,"* and paused for a few seconds before he added in his low, deeply sincere voice, *"und segne,"* pause, *"was du uns aus Gnaden"*, pause, *"bescheret"*, pause, *"hast."* pause, *"Amen."* (Come Lord Jesus, and bless what you have given us in grace. Amen.)

Sometimes when I felt sad, or needed the presence of a man, or just to be there, I grabbed a book and crossed the street into his back yard. He smiled and said, "Yah, da Billy!," clapping me on the shoulder, his warm hand resting there for a moment, filling my heart with joy.

He busied himself there, listening to German radio, the McCoys singing Christian songs, or reading a German newspaper. Or grabbing a board leaning against a sawhorse and yanking out bent nails, pounding them straight for reuse.

Often he pedaled his whetstone next to the garage, pressing the edge of a knife or hoe or other tool against the whirling wheel, sending out a river of orange sparks that curved down into the dirt. He was always doing something, perhaps to keep from being inside with Grandma Fetzer.

When he smoked, he tapped ashes into his pants cuff, his eyes took on a dreamy look, maybe remembering his own father or grandfather smoking in Russia.

Or sometimes as he read his newspaper he gazed at me with that same dreaminess. Perhaps seeing me reminded him of his childhood, triggering a foray into the past.

Sometimes he leaned forward and pedaled the whetstone furiously as though the effort might carry him back to that ancient village of his youth.

At those times he sighed and muttered as he began to weep , *"Das Schvarzes Meer, Das Schvarzes Meer,"* (The Black Sea, The Black Sea.) That chant opened a portal into his past. Judging by his mention of "Roosha," "Odessa," "Neiborg," he was speaking of his growing-up days, peering back.

I imagined him as a kid walking up and down the streets of his little Ukrainian village, gazing out at the bright sun twinkling like a million brilliant coins on the Black Sea.

Tears rolled down his cheeks, and he groaned; his heart was breaking. His eyes shimmered.

At last he wiped his tears away, and said, "Yah, da Billy," sweetly, and clapped my shoulder. He got a knife, and pressed the edge, buzzing, against the whetstone.

Sometimes when mentally in the past, he forgot what he was doing and pumped at the pedals so hard that the tool he was working on grew thin, even disintegrated.

I never understood why grief gnawed so relentlessly at the hearts of my German from Russia forebears. They had endured the persecutions of the Germans in the Ukraine, so why did Grandpa possess an insatiable desire to return where he was no longer known? Why all the *heimveih,* the home-pain, the bottomless yearning for the old country?

And he wasn't the only one in town. Occasionally during Old Prayer in church I heard "*Das Schvarzes Meer.*"

I think it symbolized belonging. We all want to belong. Need to belong. And there is no belonging so sweet, so poignant, so heartfelt, so compelling, as our earliest sense of being accepted, in the warm protective bosom of our loving first family.

As Grandpa worked, I sat nearby on a stump, leaning back against the garage, reading and at peace, a rare commodity in my life, surrounded by the soothing sounds of his gentle words or the whirling wheel or the buzzing of a knife against the stone, those mantras tolling to inform me that here was a place of sanctuary for me. Here I was safe.

Church and Religion

Failing the Commandments

The Ten Commandments didn't work for me. My disbelief stemmed from the discovery that Moses broke the first two tablets of stone which he'd brought down from Mount Sinai, "written with the finger of God." How could something from the immediate presence of God be so frail as to break when Moses flung the tablets down after waxing angry at the Israelite because they had worshiped the golden calf? Plus, if God could write on stone, surely he could wave his hand to fix the tablets instead of requiring a 90-year-old to climb the mountain for two more tablets.

Thus the Ten Commandments seemed merely old words scratched in ancient hieroglyphs on stone. Yet we were importuned to believe them. And live them. But the structure of my life meant I could not obey them.

Breaking any Commandment carried greater tonnage of sin than bad thoughts or skimming off newspaper route profits instead of handing them to my parents, as required. Or trying to get out of work that Mom wanted me to do.

I failed "Thou shalt have no other gods before me," as my coins, stamps, baseball, and searching the ravine for fossils were more important to me than God.

How could I keep the Sabbath day holy because I delivered newspapers every Sunday? If I held off until Monday, I would become an ex-paperboy.

And "Thou shalt not kill." Our mandate was *to kill* beasts that threatened farmers' crops, so I dispatched animals certainly every week, mice, rats, gophers, birds, not to mention grasshoppers, mosquitoes and other bugs.

And honoring my father? My stepdad Walter was technically my father, so I broke the fourth commandment every time I disobeyed him, called him "the old man," or flipped him the bird when he turned his back.

Then bearing false witness. Being untrue. I really didn't want to know what that meant, figuring I would find new wrongs I was already committing, another load of sins piling onto my ever-growing mound, now the size of a butte.

Thus without even trying I broke at least one a day. As the poster child for mangling commandments, I was damned, swept into a great coursing river of guilt because, try as I might, I could not obey them; could not stop sinning. I was doomed to be cast deeper into the fiery pit where the temperature burned hotter and the screams shrieked louder.

My fears were reinforced each Sunday in church by the threat of hellfire and damnation that rained down from the pulpit, reminding us that we were hopeless sinners from birth, and could never measure up to the glory of God, no matter how pure our thoughts, or how much we loved our neighbors. So why even try?

Desertion was covered, too. The weaponry to prevent us weaklings from forsaking the commandments was the threat that God could zap us with a lightning bolt at any second as an example to keep others in line.

A Visit to Hell

One day when I was eleven, Ron and I passed Scharf blacksmith shop, heading north to catch frogs. As we neared the a narrow slot of water with a slough on both sides, the mad din of frogs croaking, cheeping, thumping, peeping, and burping in bass through soprano assailed our ears.

Dozens of frogs plopped into the water, making rippling rings. As we stumbled through the thick ditch grass, the sounds diminished until a single hoarse croak of a lonely old bullfrog protested our intrusion into his domain.

The amphibians possessed no weaponry, so we stood in the slough and snatched them up one by one. They were cold and wet and slippery, but we grasped them and while they squirmed, sliced off their rear legs with jackknives honed to a sharp edge on grandpa's whetstone.

For an experiment – testing whether adult frogs regrew legs. Tadpoles regrew tails, so the concept seemed plausible. If tadpoles dropped tails when they were bitten, the tails didn't feel pain. So frog legs didn't either. So I figured.

To identify the frogs later, we tied pieces of string around their front legs and tossed them back in. After a dozen, we swished our bloody knives clean in the water, and trudged up the ditch and onto the gravel road toward home.

For food each year we killed chickens, rabbits, pigeons, and pigs and never worried that we might be hurting them. So I was shocked to discover our behavior with the frogs was cruel.

Walter yelled, "How would you like to have your legs cut off? Legs don't grow back. You really hurt those frogs."

A week later after supper we tested our hypothesis, to prove Walter wrong. Plus I felt guilty, chivied by the words of our minister last Sunday. He'd once more painted an unsettling vision of hell, the eternal pain-filled home of Satan, which lay in store for a boy like me who didn't listen to his parents, had impure thoughts, and was filled with sin.

168

"The wages of sin is death," he said. I trembled. I was destined to drop straight down into hell to burn forever in the eternal fire. Maybe even before I died! Who knew?

Grandma Fetzer's recent assaults on our front door warned that an angel would fly down from heaven, possessing the key to the bottomless pit. Grandma didn't have to say who the angel was seeking to toss down there.

The marsh did not offer any consolation. We found one dead frog with string around its arm, and no back legs, And no live ones with filament around arms. So my spirits were flagging as we headed home in the twilight.

Ed Scharf was still at work at his blacksmith shop. In the half-darkness of eventide, the spitting flames and veil of foul smoke from the doorway reminded me of hell.

The sinful guilt pressing on my fevered brain pushed me to think of Ed Scharf as the Devil incarnate, swathed in elbow-length leather gloves and heavy visor, especially when he touched his welding rod to the plow, producing a sizzling burst of bright hellfire splashing up around him, half-blinding us with its white-hot glare, even if we didn't gaze right at it..

The dazzling light reflected off the shiny plowshare, hurling frightful shadows dancing on the white walls of the building. Scharf's every movement made black images leap and quiver, like frantic gyrations of tortured souls attempting to free themselves from the torment of their sins. In the buzzing I fancied I heard the anguished cries of the damned, broiling in brimstone, with an open slot waiting for me. Too close to home.

When a nova-burst of light off the plowshare, bright as the sun, snared us in its white brilliance, painting our shadows as black flailing monsters on the road, my self-control burst, and I sprinted home, spurting gravel from beneath my soles.

The hellish scene remained etched in my memory for days.

Old Prayer

Following the calm solemnity of communion in my growing-up church, the sanctuary metamorphosed into a wild and lawless place. Passersby on the sidewalk out front could be forgiven for thinking the cries of pain, shrieks of terror, and supplications to God that they heard portended tortures applied by snapping whips, red-hot metal, or sharp knives.

They would have been partially correct, for the tortures were self-inflicted by parishioners exclaiming their sinful failings aloud.

We called it Old Prayer. "Old" because it had been passed down through time immemorial – and because it differed so much from regular prayer, needed a special name.

When time to pray was declared, everybody in the congregation rose in a body, turned around, faced the back, and knelt on the hardwood floor – no kneelers for comfort. Knee-cracking time ensued, because all over church old joints creaked and snapped. Next we leaned our elbows on the warm pew, folded our hands, pressed our thumbs against our foreheads, and with closed eyes, prayed. Out loud. In the Germans from Russia dialect. Some parishioners believed God only heard prayers in that language.

Old men with arthritic knees wrapped their arms around the whorled ends of the pews, like shipwrecked sailors who'd abandoned all hope of ever seeing land again.

Women pulled their shawls tighter over their shoulders. Like some of my friends, I didn't pray, but gazed around and study the comely girls and women, and hope for a glimpse of a thigh in a hiked-up skirt. More sinning.

Old Prayer began in silence. Seconds later whispers wafted like a gentle prairie breeze. Moments later low mutterings started, a jumble of voices incoherent and indistinct, like faint rumbling of thunder.

Slowly voices grew louder, quivering up into falsetto, the drizzle of words becoming clear and plaintive – *"Jesus, was mar getup hat?"* (Jesus, what have I done?) And "*Verger mir Herr,"* (Forgive me Lord) and "*Ich have niche Geller an intelligentsia Eben,"* (I have not lived a good life.)

More voices joined in, increasing the intensity, louder still and faster, a shower pelting from all directions – "*Gott der Herr,"* "*Ich Weiss nit,"* "*Wen sie wills,"* (God you are the Lord,) (I don't know,) (Your will be done.)

Lightning flashes of high-pitched wailing and keening of indescribable loss, dark words of *heimveih* (home pain) people desperately missing that other place in the old country, *Das Schvarzes Meer,* which still held them in thrall.

And yet more. The storm rose in fury, a frenzied, ululating wail of quavering voices like pummeling hailstones, obliterating each other; a frenzied Tower of Babel, interspersed with heart-rending sobs, and massive sighs and groans.

Grandpa Fetzer clutched the top end of the pew, praying aloud in a high-pitched German voice, wailing as he repeated his sins, his hands clenched fiercely in front of him, wiping his eyes and blowing his nose on his hanky.

When I peered over the back of my pew and gazed at all these poor sailors adrift in the sea of life, I was overwhelmed by the tears streaming down their faces, and their cries of pain. I was also astounded. These innocent-looking men and women that I knew to be good people were admitting grievous sins of straying from the ways of the Lord, general sins I could not imagine them committing.

After fifteen minutes of wildness, a crescendo, a crash, a thunder of voices, and the sobs lessened; the crying subsided into whimpering; the voices lowered into whispers, and sometimes I would hear someone ask God to guide Billy, the wayward servant, to keep him on the straight and narrow, to forge him into a sharp sacred sword of the Lord.

Then came heartfelt, fervent amens from every corner of the church. The great storm was over. With sighs and moans and blowing of noses and mopping of eyes and creaking of joints, Old Prayer for an old people from an old country yearning for an old way of life forever lost, was over.

Potatoes

Grumberra Chronicles

It seemed to me that the plot of land a block from home existed to destroy my serenity. Day, night, tide, time, the parcel reminded me that another stage loomed in the chain of work of raising *Grumberra* (potatoes).

I passed that level landscape at least four times a day, to and from delivering newspapers, to and from school, and sometimes to and from uptown. Every time – every time! – the view of that acreage, showing a white blanket of snow, or smooth brown dirt with a few dead volunteer sprouts, or humped with ridges from the planted tubers, or teeming with green potato plants, or pockmarked with holes, all warned me that the next stage in the unrelenting year-long battle against potatoes would begin again all too soon.

Turning my eyes away was no use, as I then imagined I could hear the remnants of the roots of potato plants of yesteryear whispering, "Won't be long now until they thrust our cousins down here once more with us. Hooray!"

The assault began in winter in the basement bin, precipitated when someone grabbed a fistful of tubers out of the dark pile to take up for supper, and one exploded in their hand, spewing stinky wet ooze onto their fingers and dribbling down onto other potatoes in the bin. If me, the smell made me gag.

Worse, all potatoes in the bin had to be examined, because that bad one, nicked by the digging fork, or tossed carelessly into a pail, had been slowly going putrid, and if not removed could have infected others. If all the bad ones were not removed, the entire binful could be corrupted, inedible.

That would be disaster for our family who depended heavily on potatoes: mashed, roasted, fried, potato pies, potato pancakes, *kartoffel und klobble*, (potatoes and dumplings), strudels, potato salads, French fries, stews, and on and on.

So after finding a bad one, several of us hoisted a pile of potatoes out and placed them on the floor, or table, and inspected them one by one, turning them this way and that, as though searching for treasure. Each potato needed to be squeezed. No one had to ask, "Did you find a bad one?" as "Ewww!" would ring along with the powerful odor cascading through the basement.

Each tuber that had touched ooze had to be washed and dried to prevent reinfection. Potatoes had to be checked before spring anyway, but it was much better without oozes.

Despite living in the dark basement, the potatoes sensed enough brightness filtering down to raise their hopes, so they shunted pale roots from their eyes, nubbins to inches long, poking out for light, and growth. We twisted them off so they didn't eat up the food inside that a new plant needed to grow.

Just one step in the never-ending list of steps of growing potatoes.

Cutting Up

In the sanctuary of my dream, I scuffed the dirt away from home plate with my spikes, and stood in the batter's box. The pitcher wound up. I swung and smacked the pitch with the sweet part of the bat. Thousands of howling fans in Yankee Stadium leaped to their feet, roaring as the white ball soared up and away, over the right field fence and into the bleachers, winning the World Series.

I had just stepped on first base on my home run trot when "*Schteig oof!*" (Get up!) jolted me awake, my stepdad yelling down to our warm bed in our basement room. "*Grumberra* (potatoes) won't plant themselves, and today is the day. So *Schteig oof!* (Get up!)" I glanced at the dark window. The sun had not yet risen. But my two brothers and I pried ourselves out of bed and got dressed.

I groaned. From a great high to a terrible low. Another spring Saturday ruined with work. I was twelve and hated being forced to rise before cockcrow to gulp a bowl of Wheaties and head to work I despised, this time planting potatoes. I wasn't fond of any work at any time, not when I could be playing baseball or hunting fossils or fiddling with my stamp collection.

I grumbled as I shambled across the street to Grandpa Fetzer's, momentarily buoyed by the dew sparkling in the dried grass and the long moving shadows from the barely-risen sun.

Preparing the seed was the next step in the year-long work of planting potatoes. In the basement Grandpa clapped me on the shoulder and said, "Yah, da Billy!" He glanced at the mountain of tubers. "*Grumberra,*" (potatoes) he said, smiling. We grabbed knives he had whetted on his pedal millstone in the back yard, grabbed a potato, noted the eyes, and pressed the knife through the sphere to thump into the wooden table below, and reveal the yellow-white interior of the soon-to-be-seed.

Each planted chunk required at least one eye, using the meat to nurture the young plants. For a moment I considered cutting out all the eyes of my potatoes so no plants would grow. Fewer plants, less future work.

But with six other people whittling at the great pile, my efforts would be useless. Plus Mom would discover my perfidy by the blank potatoless rows where I'd planted, and I would not only catch heck, but additional punitive work later, and what would we eat?

As we worked, the pile dwindled, and a gunnysack bulged larger with eyed pieces we tossed in, unworried about bruising them now. When only a couple of rows remained in the bottom of the bin, enough for Grandma's summer cooking, we grabbed the bag and empty one-gallon Karo syrup pails and trudged up the hill towards our garden plot while shivering sparrows and robins chirped among the thin leaves in the cottonwoods.

We owned the largest garden in town. The dark earth extended from the narrow crumbling sidewalk along the street, a half block across to the alley, 150 by 100 feet, plus a twenty by thirty-foot garden behind our house. We raised carrots, onions, beets, lettuce, cabbage, peas, beans, cucumbers, pumpkins, watermelons, and strawberries.

And potatoes. Miles of potatoes. Or so it seemed.

Plowing and Planting

At the garden we filled the pails with sliced potatoes from the gunnysack, while the distant sound of a tractor grew louder. Old Man Becker drove up in a little gray Fordson, chugged over the curb, across the boulevard, and onto the verge of the garden.

We waited while Mom and Walter spoke to him in German, and I tried to figure out a way to avoid this work. I could act sick, but they wouldn't believe me. If only they had provided advance notice...

When Becker puttered to the corner of the garden, it signaled each of us to move to our planting areas, marked off on the side of the garden by laths pounded in the ground. Becker stopped and glanced back at the single gleaming plowshare dangling a couple of feet above the ground. He slid the transmission into gear, lowered the plow, roared the engine, and motored ahead.

The steel-bright plow sliced smoothly into the earth, rolling a burnished wide layer of soil off to the side, creating a furrow. Our signal. Shivering, I grabbed my pail, the handle cold against my bare fingers, and fumbled for a handful of moist potato chunks. They poked out between my fingers like white tumors.

When the plow passed, I stepped into the fresh furrow, and plunged a potato wedge with the eye up wrist-deep into the bottom of the damp earth turned by the steel. Soil and stones scraped my hands, but the sweet essence of the earth enveloped me, the smell of life itself, and reminded me of past plantings in this garden. This process had been repeated by my forebears countless times hankering back to the Ukraine, and eons earlier in Germany. But before I could dream of my caveman ancestors, I was called to task.

I bent and stabbed in another, and another, and another, each a foot further down the furrow from its fellow. The black soil gobbled up the white slices, until I reached the end of my planting zone. Only a thousand rows to go! My hands began to grow numb, and so did my brain.

The tractor paused at the far end of the furrow and snatched the plowshare out of the dark earth, so it bounced like a live beast, shedding clots of dirt. All along the newly-turned soil wriggling earthworms were exposed, catching the attention of robins and seagulls waiting impatiently in the air and in trees so when we weren't nearby they could dart down and eat.

All of us stepped out of the rut as the tractor, leaning drunkenly with one tire in the furrow, roared backwards, and as it passed me the whir of its radiator fan slapped my face with a welcome blast of warm engine air. The tractor paused at the beginning of the next row, lowered the plow, and leaped forward once more, curling soil atop where the newly-planted potatoes had been stabbed in the ground, and creating a fresh new furrow ready to receive more tubers from my potato-filled fingers.

So it went, row after row. Bored between planting stints, I began to search for trinkets in the soil that piqued my interest – colored stones, chips of flint, pieces of crockery, a couple of rusty nails and screws – and then I spotted an unusual circle of dirt. Perfectly round. I held my breath and picked it up. I rubbed the dirt off between my thumb and forefinger – and gasped.

The real world dimmed. I became oblivious to the voices of my family, the chirps of the birds, and the roar of the tractor. I saw only – a coin. An old buried coin. But how old? And what kind? Greek drachma? Roman Darius? Spanish piece of eight? The words were as sweetly evocative as a coin might be.

I spit on the coin and wiped it clean on my jeans, revealing the beautiful profile of an Indian on the front. The face was as detailed as the day the planet had been stamped in the United States Mint decades earlier. The feathers in the headdress were perfect too, as well as the "United States of America" in raised letters near the rim.

177

And then most incredibly, the date. 1881! The reverse showed ONE CENT surrounded by a wreath wrapped around pointed arrows. An Indian head penny! I was ecstatic!

"Billy!" my mother yelled, "*Gook aus!*" (Look out!)

Engrossed as I was, I hadn't noticed the tractor bearing down on me in reverse. Its rear wheel brushed my thigh and knocked me back.

"*Schteig oof!* (Wake up!) What's wrong with you?"

Wrong? I rubbed the penny, joy cascading through me. How could anything be wrong?

I slid the penny into my pants pocket, where it seemed to burn. From then on I planted at super-speed, freeing time to sift and search for more coins.

"Are you feeling okay?" Mom said, studying me.

Of course I was okay. I'd found buried treasure! How could I not be okay? I didn't show her what I'd found, fearing repercussions that I was looking for old money and not working hard enough.

Which was probably accurate, as after that, anything vaguely circular became another possible piece of buried treasure: stones, more pieces of glass, buttons, roots, and clods of earth.

Over the next few years my treasure hunt in the garden yielded six more: an 1898 Liberty Head nickel, 1903 Standing Liberty quarter, and four more Indianhead pennies dating to the early 1900s.

The discoveries produced a mystery: how did the coins get buried in the garden? Part of a larger undiscovered horde? Was the area a former walking path? Even an old business? I never solved it.

Regardless, the coins were gifts making me wide-eyed with wonder, and for our family, I suppose, because I could truthfully say with astonishment that now after spending years trying to avoid work, I looked forward to seeing the soil turned while planting potatoes every year, so I could search for more buried treasure.

Potato Wars

For a few days after planting day, Mom and Walter failed to assign any other work, knowing a full slate of upcoming potato work would soon pin me down for much of the rest of the summer. Up until then, each day after I finished delivering papers, freedom resounded, and I indulged my every desire: fossils, baseball, slingshot shooting, minnow hunting, reading, the entire array of favorite pastimes.

Meanwhile gentle raindrops dribbled into the soil and tapped the newly-planted immersed potato pieces on their shoulders, reminding them to grow. And they did, poking up shyly through the soil, nudging aside tiny lumps of dirt as they sought sunlight. But weeds also flourished – creeping jenny, crab grass, dandelions, knapweed – stealing moisture and gobbling up the potatoes' food.

Clearly the next mission my parents set for my brothers and me was to annihilate the weeds. We crawled down the long rows, our knees pressing into the warm soil, flinching when sharp hidden rocks pressed against our kneecaps. Amid the dusky smell of the earth in the field that seemed to stretch out forever, we yanked out weeds until our fingers ached. We did our duty, which was to protect the tiny delicate shoots of the potato plants.

But more weeds seemed to shoot up instantly in our knee-dents behind us as we forged ahead. When we were finished with dozens of rows, we turned around and began again, so the pulled-up dead weeds couldn't reseed. When we finished weeding, I looked forward to hard-earned time off.

But potatoes didn't allow time off. Next we took hoes and mounded dirt around the base of each plant to protect the roots from torrential rains, blasting winds, and the unrelenting summer sun which seemed to beat down the hottest it seemed during our hours of servitude.

Mounding dirt took time. Each stalk had to be dealt with individually, pushing dirt toward the plant from every direction until the mound grew large enough to protect it. Care was required to avoid nipping the roots with the hoe, lessening the number of new potatoes to be born, or killing the plant. The mounding seemed to take days, but unlike other potato work, needed to be done only once a year, thank God.

Even when a thunderstorm or high winds or tornado weather struck, providing a day off, I couldn't enjoy the freedom. My browned arms, calloused fingers, and dirt-encrusted shoes reminded me of the labor I'd already done, and more to be done remained lodged in the back of my mind, a landslide teetering at the top of a mountain.

As soon as the mounding was finished, potato bugs surfaced in the never-ending battle of the unending potato wars. They appeared as though our hoes had opened pathways from the ground to release them. I tried to convince mom of the truth of that, hoping to cut down on my work, but she was having none of it. Suddenly all sizes of the little beasts materialized, eggs to adults, hiding on the underside of the green leaves, munching away. I couldn't skip any plants because their insect-eaten condition would reveal my laziness, and I would catch heck.

While I poured a few inches of kerosene into a coffee can, I wondered: Where did the potato bugs come from? How did they know when to come? Why in our garden? What did they eat before they started on potato plants?

With the can of kerosene in one hand, I bent over one plant at a time, lifting each soft spongy leaf, searching for jelly-like masses of golden yellow eggs, which I scraped off into the can. Chubby half-inch larva went too. Looking like small over-stuffed pieces of red-orange sausage with a head, they seemed harmless, but when they nibbled leaves they robbed chlorophyll and life from the plants. I flicked the larvae into the kerosene, or skimmed them off the leaves into the can, where they piled atop of the bodies on the bottom.

Few adult beetles existed, due to our early-and-frequent searches for the pests. The hard-shelled adults were

180

light yellow with ten black stripes on their backs from head to end, larvae we had missed during earlier hunting forays. Adults were plunked into the kerosene preventing them from doing extra damage.

During the hunts I distracted myself by searching for the buggiest plants: "Seven larvae here, plus one adult and eggs!" I tried to find the buggiest row, too. But the rows were long, I was hot, uncomfortable and frustrated, and I kept searching for more old coins, which broke my concentration, so I never finished the count of any row.

Even at night potatoes haunted me. I dreamt that the garden had been overrun with high weeds strangling the plants. And swarms of red bugs teemed and nibbled off the leaves, stripping every plant naked.

As summer edged towards the dog days in August, the next chore was to push a three-pronged cultivator up and down between the rows of plants, upending a few hardy weeds, but more importantly, loosening the soil so the potatoes could thrive, we were told.

About this same time, the bin in our basement moved toward empty, so Mom sent me up to the garden to dig a hill or two of potatoes. The sun was hot and I sweated, flies droning, mosquitoes buzzing and biting, the distant sounds of the town wafting through the air as I retrieved the potatoes. I grimaced, reminded of the hard work of harvesting yet to come.

And that day did come, another Saturday which allowed everybody to be available. No tractor needed now. Just human power. Several of us were tapped to pull up the plants. That took skill, but at twelve my folks figured I knew how, as I had watched how they withdrew the plant so the fewest potatoes broke loose and stayed underground.

Mom watched me as I grabbed my first stalk, feeling its dried sharpness against my palm. Noting resistance, I pulled up slowly and carefully, allowing the treasures to rise out of the ground. Eight fat dirty potatoes dangled off the roots, round and bulging, hanging like a child's mobile.

For as much as I had fought working with potatoes, for a moment I gazed at them with pride. I was one of the reasons they had grown so well. Plenty to get us through the winter.

I pulled off the potatoes, and put them on the ground. I stuck the fork in the hole where the plant had grown, and stirred it around, unearthing two more. I must have passed the test, as Mom bent back to her work.

Certain that no more potatoes were hidden at that spot, I pushed dirt back into the hole, and moved to the next plant. I pulled it up, revealing another set of hanging potatoes. My brother picked up the potatoes I'd dug up, placed them carefully in a pail, so they wouldn't bruise, and then with care slipped them into a gunnysack.

After an hour or so, we rotated work so I picked up potatoes too. When we were finished with the garden, hot sweaty hours later, the plot looked like a war scene, lumps of dirt all around, the plants flung about like dead soldiers. I had survived, and I breathed a sigh of relief.

With our Radio Flyer I helped transport the gunnysacks, most to our basement bin a block away, some to Grandpa and Grandma Fetzer's, and a couple to Mrs. Sayler as rent for the use of her land.

I began to admit to the value of hard work and doing a job well. I knew I would never be free of potatoes: reminded every day passing the garden, bringing up potatoes from the bin, eating them, seeing the digging fork and three-pronged cultivator in the chicken coop poised and ready for the next season.

I also learned that the earth never changed. Most of the footfalls and hoe marks and cultivator lines and tine holes etched into that field would disappear by the next time the Fordson showed up, as though we had never been there. The landscape would look as it had a hundred years ago.

Ervin and Baseball

My Love of Baseball

Regulars at Woehl Stadium included my cousin Jim Woehl, Ervin Gall, and Randy Eckman.

The love of baseball coursed through my veins from the day of my birth. In the maternity ward of Deaconess Hospital in Billings where I was born in the summer of 1946, I doubtless heard the cheers of the crowds at Athletic Park three blocks away.

When Mom stepped out of the car, cradling me in her arms as she headed to our fourplex, I could have imprinted the crack of baseballs off the bats of the Billings Mustangs rookie league team, because we lived right across the street from Athletic Park.

183

When I was a tyke, Mom took me across the street to the stadium to prevent me from crossing by myself. She sat on the grass as I stood with my fingers laced through the wire fence, watching the Mustangs take batting practice, or the American Legion baseball teams play, hearkening to the cries of the players and the sacred sounds of the balls against the bats, crying with joy when the white orbs soared.

In Wishek Mom married Walter Delzer, an avid baseball fan who taught me how to play the game when I was seven. Walter's brother Howard stood behind me with both hands on the handle of the bat above mine, guiding my swing while Walter prepared to lob the ball.

"No, no," Walter said, "Billy is left-handed. He bats from the left side."

Left-handed! My mouth fell open. That meant I was different! Special!

My love for the game blossomed. Like Walter, I loved the Yankees, and I played every chance I got.

But places to play baseball in Wishek were limited. The main diamond was twelve blocks distant and always in use with organized teams. So friends and I began to play uptown in a small vacant lot next to Ketterling Cream Station, imagining ourselves as our baseball heroes, pitching and fielding and smacking the ball amidst the cries of "safe" or "out" or "home run" echoing through the neighborhood.

Until we rocketed too many balls across the street onto lawns and flower beds. When a couple of shots bounced off siding near picture windows, our days there were numbered. We were scared of having to pay, so we needed a bigger diamond.

I was in the midst of a great dream. I believed with every fiber of my being that I was grooming for a career as a major-league baseball player to replace Mickey Mantle in center field at Yankee Stadium. So we needed more than a mere baseball diamond; we needed a stadium.

That stadium would be appropriate to our rising station in life, preparing us for standing at attention along the white-chalked first-base line in Yankee Stadium, our caps stitched with red NY held over our hearts as the strains of the "Star-Spangled Banner" echoed in the cavernous depths.

We found an empty lot next to my cousin Jim Woehl's garage. My imagination ran wild. In my mind's eye I envisioned a finished stadium with an outfield fence; a pitcher's mound; chalked foul lines; sand around the bases and base paths; a bullpen; a backstop – and a double-decker stadium, seats filled with cheering fans. Why not?

We cut the high grass, releasing the sweet smell of new-mown hay, *marravarich*, and an hour later, sweaty but energized, we set down bases: part of a car-tire tube, old yellow stop sign, square of cardboard, and wood for home plate.

Amidst the joy of a job well done, with competition singing in our veins – we chose sides, and played our first game in Woehl Stadium.

Though we had to use weathered bats with splinters nailed back on with sticky black electrical tape wound around, balls restitched with fish line filament, ancient gloves tattered and torn, caps sweat-stained and dirty, we felt like kings with new equipment.

Many kids played at Woehl Stad-ium, like Del Eisenbeis, batting.

185

Building a Baseball Stadium

As the summer moved on, I felt we needed more stadium improvements. First, a dugout. Thus we shoveled out a six-foot-long rectangle of dirt to the east side of the diamond, sliced off one long side of cardboard from a Kelvinator refrigerator box, and slid the rest of the box into the two-foot-deep and three-foot-wide hole. Bingo! A dugout. A hole in the floor, covered with wood, housed a burlap bag with our few bats and balls and gloves, keeping them always available.

Then baselines to first and third, and a bullpen, with the grass cut. Next a raised pitcher's mound.

But since we regularly lacked enough players for a catcher – the batter had to chase missed pitches, delaying the game – we pounded wooden posts into the ground three feet behind home plate and nailed chicken wire to them. Missed balls struck the wire and rolled down the slope to the feet of the batter. Perfect!

The beginning of a professional baseball stadium. I was proud and elated! I imagined a scoreboard, baselines, outfield fence – everything.

Also professional score sheets. I'd worked for the school janitor and knew the location of the ditto machine in the basement of the high school, and had seen a teacher operate it. I also knew the back door was often unlocked during the summer.

After delivering newspapers one day, I slipped in the back door of the high school and dashed down to the machine, where I found a box of ditto masters. I stole two of them.

At home I used a ruler to draw two baseball score sheets, one with the New York Yankee lineup listed, the other with blanks.

The next day I biked back to school. I took a deep breath and pulled open the back door. Tiptoed down the

186

steps. Much more dangerous now because I'd be creating a racket using the machine. What excuse could I offer if I was caught? "Hi, I'm making baseball score sheets, using school equipment and stealing paper." Mom would have a conniption if I got caught.

I stopped and listened. Silence.

At the machine it took me a minute to figure out how to attach the ditto master to the drum. Listened again. Silence, except for the beating of my heart. I grabbed the handle and turned the drum. Nothing happened. Glanced over. Empty paper tray.

I opened the double doors of the gray metal cabinet below. Eureka! New reams of paper – and a can labeled "duplicating fluid." Oops. If the machine was empty of fluid, I was in real trouble.

I slid paper into the tray. Listened. No footsteps, no voices, no doors slamming. Nothing.

I cranked the drum – and a copy of my Yankees' score sheet appeared. Yay! But while making thirty copies the noise boomed and echoed. How could the whole world not hear? I was breathing hard.

Changed the masters.

Listened – still okay. Dittoed thirty score sheets with blank spaces. Piled them all together. Smelled them. Headed up the stairs fast. Silently as I could.

Halfway up, I stopped. The masters! Damn! I was tempted to leave them. Who would know I had made them?

Then I heard the click of the outer door upstairs. Voices of two men. Yeep! But lucky me. I'd have been nailed for sure if not for remembering the masters. But I was still in trouble.

I turned back, leaning on the railing to leap three steps at a time. Score sheets started coming loose. Grappled at them before they fell.

Needed a hiding place. Looked desperately around. Not much available. Crouched down behind the cabinet with the ditto machine.

Heard feet clump on the stairs. My goose was cooked! My heart nearly jumped out of my chest. More footsteps! Prison for sure. More footsteps.

But I realized they were not coming nearer. They were receding. Going up to the second floor. Held my breath.

Waited a few more seconds. Blew out my breath. Poked my head out. Nobody. Glanced up the steps. Nobody. Ran to the stairs. Remembered the masters. Ran back. Grabbed them. Raced up the stairs, flinging caution aside. Nobody yelled, "Billy Vossler, what are you doing here?" Or, "what are those sheets you're holding?"

Like a criminal, I raced outside. Dropped the score sheets and masters in my bike basket. Hopped on. Pedaled away hard. No cries of "thief!" No police sirens. Safe!

I used the Yankee score sheets for my team, with dual names: "Bill Vossler/Mickey Mantle." The opposing team had only their real names of the other Wishek guys on the sheet.

Surprisingly, the names of my team's players paired with Yankee players often performed like the professionals did in American League games – my teammate slotted in singles-hitter Bobby Richardson's batting spot most often singled, while the player in home run hitter Mickey Mantle's spot often hit homers. For a while I tallied up at-bats and hits and batting averages.

Using the score sheets lasted only a few weeks, as Ervin and I were the only ones interested – a huge comedown for me considering the dangers I'd encountered to make them. That's when I began to realize that my friends' ideas and mine for playing baseball differed.

Meeting Ervin

I met Ervin Gall when I was a sixth-grader, ready to play basketball with four others in an alley one winter day. He showed up just as we needed a sixth player to make a pair of three-on-three teams.

Afterwards, if someone had told me Ervin would have a major positive effect on my life, I would have thought them "*verrucht*," or "crazy."

I'd had little interest in basketball before then. But I became desperate to learn the game because my arch-enemy for the attention of certain girls was playing basketball with the older kids because "He was so good," a classmate said. That provided him with extra cachet with the girls, and left me out in the cold. So I tried to work into their good graces.

Six of us shoveled the snow off the court and piled it high along the edges of the small playing area. As we worked I wondered why this hulk of a man was playing with middle school kids. Not a question to ask right then.

He was five-ten, rock-solid, and muscular with broad shoulders and strong hands that wrested the ball away from us twerps. He was obviously twenty years older, and during our scrimmage, I began to realize that he was also different. Physically, but also mentally.

As we played, Ervin stood rooted beneath the basket like a giant oak tree with arms, grabbing rebounds with his strong hands, laughing a high-pitched "Hee hee hee," struggling against us runts trying to steal the ball.

Grunting and laughing, "Hee hee hee," he raised the ball over his head to shoot, sometimes with one of us clutching it, or his arm, but he held tightly to the ball even while hoisting us off our feet until we slid off.

He banged the ball two-handed off the backboard, making it quiver, grabbing the sphere again, flinging it until he made the basket or fired it so hard that it bounced to someone else.

189

All the while he laughed "Hee hee hee" in a high happy voice.

As we played more games with Ervin that winter, we realized he was too strong for us. If we wanted to win, we had to be underhanded. We had to try to punch the ball away with our fists – but it proved useless – no amount of battering loosened it from his powerful grip. He merely laughed, his teeth gleaming under eyes filled with delight.

Or we jerked his cap down over his eyes, hoping he would forget about the ball for a couple of seconds, but to no avail. He clenched it tightly and said, "Haaaay," adjusted his cap and shot the ball.

One time a loose ball bounced out of bounds towards a huge pile of snow. Several of us dived after it, attempting to save it for our team, but also for the joy of leaping into a snow pile. When we were down, Ervin lunged on top of us, crushing us into the snow, and with his arms spread across us, muttering, "I just luff you guys."

I learned to love Ervin too. Not out of pity when I discovered that at twelve he fell off a high stack of bales, and struck his skull on the sharp corner of the hayrack below, forever stalling his brain in junior high, but because of his effervescent personality despite his handicap, his friendliness, his joy of life. He was always ready with a smile, always happy.

Ervin's Big Home Run

Ervin was my friend until we were with girls I wanted to impress. Once two girls I liked walked by on the gravel road by the stadium, and stopped to chat. Ervin drooled and stuttered and laughed, "Hee hee hee," several times – just being Ervin, really. That irked me. When he said, "Biddee and I are friends," I worried the girls thought less of me for having a friend with developmental issues.

Later that day when I prepared to pitch to Ervin, my anger rushed back. Why did he swing the bat so weirdly, like a tomahawk instead of across the plate like the rest of us, the right way? When he pitched, why did he wind up like the old pitchers in the 1920s? He invited people to make fun of him.

He pounded his bat on the plate. "Haaay! Rubber arm!" he cried. "Hum chucka, baby! Just try to-to-to throw a strike in here. Haaay! You-you-you don't know how to throw strikes. We want a pitcher, Biddee, not a glass of water. Hee hee hee! Haaay!"

Normally those insults, picked up from town team baseball, meant nothing. Today I took them personally. I felt the rough horsehide against my fingers. Time to get even.

I wound up, reared back, and fired a fast ball high and tight. At his head. Ervin squinched his eyes, grunted, and swung his bat over his head straight down, as though he was clubbing the ground.

Usually his hits dribbled into the infield. Not this time. Crack!

"Whoa!" someone cried. Our heads turned. The ball rose over the infield, soared higher and higher over the outfielders, across the road, and plopped into Gutschmidt's rhubarb patch.

Ervin's first home run ever! A monster blast! Our jaws dropped. He hippity-hopped around the bases like a little kid. We mobbed him at home, and for a moment I forgot I was mad at him and half-hugged him.

After his team made the third out, I attempted to mark HR on the score sheet by Ervin's name, but he locked his big paw on my wrist so I couldn't write. His eyes were large as new baseballs and he panted and hopped back and forth like a little kid needing the bathroom.

"Biddee!" he said. "Biddee! I hit-I hit-I hit-I hit a home run."

"I know, Ervin."

"Biddee!"

"Yes, Ervin."

"I hit-I hit-"

"Yes, Ervin, I know!"

"Biddee, Biddee, how far?"

I had marked my longest home run with a Popsickle stick in the garden across the road, moving it each time I hit one further.

"How far, Biddee?"

I thought I knew how far – farther than mine. I would be known as the pitcher who not only gave up Ervin's first home run ever – probably the only one he would ever hit – and a blast hit farther than mine. What if the Yankees found out? I felt heartsick.

"Pretty far," I said, glancing at the others, a couple grinning as they mimicked Ervin's swing. I snatched up a ball and hid it in my hand in the folds of my shirt at my hip. "Let's go see how far," I said. Someone always had to retrieve home runs.

Laughter dogged us across the outfield, maybe directed toward me for giving up the homer. Maybe for Ervin. He stammered and asked why others made fun of him.

"I don't know, Ervin," I said, feeling uneasy.

"I-I-I don't do anything to them, Biddee. Why do they want to hurt me?"

I fidgeted as we crossed the gravel road into the garden. "Sometimes if you make fun of someone else, it makes you feel better. For a little bit, I guess."

192

While he gazed into the distance, I released the ball I'd hidden. The thump made me jump.

"It-it-it-" He slapped his chest with his palm, and a tear trickled out of his eye. His face turned soft. "That-that-that's why I like you, Biddee," he said. "You wouldn't do that to me."

I blanched, and averted my eyes. With forced heartiness I said, "Look Ervin!" and made a show of discovering the ball I'd just planted. "Your home run ball! Almost as far as mine!"

He took it. "Oh no, Biddee," he said. "That's not my ball."

Uh-oh, I thought. The jig's up. I glanced wildly around, then hung my head. Softly I said "Maybe you're right, Ervin. Maybe the ball hit somewhere else." My heart sank. I wished I'd brought another ball to plant. But I hadn't. Time to be honest. "Oh yeah," I pointed. "Over there. I remember now."

Looking at the ball in his hand, Ervin said, "This is your new ball. We don't want to use it yet, remember? It's too nice." He showed me Mickey Mantle's blue handwriting next to the red seams. My hero. Not the Yankee outfielder's actual handwritten signature, but duplicated. Yet still special to me.

I grabbed the ball, and stalked to my Popsicle stick thrust in the earth. And past. I rummaged among the rhubarb, and found a baseball. "Here's your ball."

Ervin's eyes measured his home run and my stake. "Oh n-no, Biddee. I couldn't have hit it that far. Not farther than you." He shook his head.

"You did."

"No, Biddee, not farther than your ball."

With the heel of my shoe I gouged a line in the soft earth. "Yes," I said. "Here's where we'll put your stake." I smiled with relief. Honesty felt good.

Ervin rubbed out the line with his boot. "No."

"Yes. You hit it, Ervin. Fair and square. You deserve it." He tried to say no, but was pleased. He started crying.

"And as a prize," I said, as he blubbered softly, I pried open his thick hand and stuck my baseball into it.

"But Biddee! This is the wrong ball!"

"No it isn't."

"But oh no, The Mick's name is on it! It-it's yours!"

"Now it's yours, Ervin. I closed his fingers over the ball and held them shut. "It's a trade."

"A-a-a trade? For what, Biddee? I don't have..."

I held his arm. "For..." I couldn't say "For helping me be honest." Instead, more truthfully, I said, "For-for being my friend."

Friends Forever

One evening that wondrous summer, in the magical fading orange rays of the sun, Ervin and I met at Woehl Stadium to prick our fingers with a needle and mix our blood to declare our friendship, like Huck and Tom in *The Adventures of Tom Sawyer*.

While the mourning doves cooed their lonely songs, we pledged an eternal oath: "We will always be friends," we whispered. "We will always be together. Even as Yankees."

"Or-or-or Dodgers," Ervin said.

At the last moment my sticking-courage failed me – a harbinger – so I didn't pull the needle out of my pocket and told Ervin it would work just as well if we used spit.

We spat in our hands, rubbed them together, incanting "Friends forever," several times, lifting an index finger as a secret signal. Ervin seemed deeply moved by the ritual. "Always friends?" He kept asking. "Always together?"

As night fell, in choked voices we said goodbyes and wended our ways home to sleep contentedly. Life was perfect.

The next day Ervin was pitching. I smacked the ball on the sweet part of the bat, scalding a line drive at Ervin.

Splat! In the crotch! He toppled like a sawed-off redwood. The ball trickled away. I rushed to his side, peering at his pale face. Someone picked up the ball and tagged me. "You're out!" he said triumphantly. "Three down. We're up!"

Ervin's eyes rolled back. "Ervin," I cried, "Ervin!" I patted him on the cheek. Nothing. Was he dead?

Until then I hadn't realized how much I prized his friendship. But he was dead. A moment later he groaned. "Ervin!" I cried, relieved beyond measure, "you're alive!"

I flopped onto his strong chest. He gasped, wheezing, while I thumped him in glad wonder. His hands were clasped on his groin. Color returned to his face. He opened his eyes,

He smiled painfully, and spluttered, "Ooooh, Biddee," he said, "you hit that one good, hee hee hee!"

The Firecracker Incident

After playing baseball one day in early July, I was standing in the outfield musing to Ervin about batters' boxes and baselines lined with chalk, real bases instead of pieces of wood, an outfield fence – all like the professionals. And heck, a giant scoreboard in center field too. Why not?

A player who seldom showed up was very animated that day. He produced a pack of a hundred blood-red ladyfinger firecrackers, and I smiled. Firecrackers were popping all over town.

He stood behind Ervin, and grinned at me, holding up the package in one hand, and a farmer's match in the other. He pointed at the firecrackers, the match, and Ervin.

Someone whispered, "You keep Ervin talking. We'll do the rest."

I frowned. "The rest? What?" I said, slow on the uptake, because I couldn't believe people would think of doing something like that. I should have yelled, "No, not to my friend!"

The guy with the firecrackers slipped the entire package of ladyfingers into Ervin's back pocket. I smelled a stab of sulfur. Fuses hissed.

"Noooo!" I said, too late.

"Haaaaay!" Ervin whirled. "What-what's-what's going on back there?"

The first firecracker blew, followed by crackity crack crack, then a cacophony like a single sound.

Ervin leaped and slapped at his rump. A couple of guys laughed triumphantly. A knife twisted in my gut. But due to the awkward leap and the perplexed look, I laughed too.

As though someone had sliced his jugular, the color drained from Ervin's face. Shreds of paper with alien writing hung in the air. The silence was cold and wide as winter.

Ervin didn't scream, "You traitors!" as he should have. He didn't look at the others. His eyes sought mine, and held up a single index finger. Twin wet trails appeared on his cheeks.

"Erv!" I croaked.

He flung down his glove and ran, his shredded pocket hanging down and bobbing behind him. Someone yelled "Ergy Burp," a name he despised.

Minutes later Ervin's family accosted us. His father, mother, and older brother had red spots high on their angry cheeks. We stood mutely, knowing we had done wrong. They shielded Ervin behind them as they screeched at us, words and spittle flying, "Terrible, awful. You know Ervin isn't right. You shouldn't take advantage of him. If you don't know better, you should!"

I did know better, and I felt awful, but I didn't have the courage to protest as I should have.

Ervin Shows Me How to Be a Friend

Following the firecrackers incident, I stumbled on in darkness for several days, wanting to get back in Ervin's good graces. I walked past his house on the way to play baseball, hoping he would see me and step out onto the stairs and say, "Hi, Biddee," and laugh, or show up at the field so I could apologize. But he didn't. And a couple players were elated that Ervin wasn't playing.

"Now we have guys who know how to play baseball," someone said.

A few days later on a misty afternoon my heart was thumping as I walked the two blocks toward Ervin's house. On the way I studied the drops of water hanging off the edges of the leaves of the pigweeds, reflections of me as I walked past pools, and how the houses looked in the half-fog, because I knew if I thought about going to Ervin's, I would lose courage.

I made straight for his house and climbed the steps and knocked on the front door. Drops of water streaked down from the sills of the small windows, like tears down a cheek. I knocked again, harder, planning to apologize.

Ervin's brother Noyal tore the door open, and glowered at me. He hissed, "He doesn't want to see you or any of you guys. So get the hell out of here. You ain't no good for him. Leave him alone." He slammed the door.

I raised my fist to knock again, but lowered it and turned away, walking slowly home in the rain.

A couple of days later before going to the post office to get my newspapers, I waited in the morning shadows beneath the soaring trees down the block from Ervin's place. His father and brother hitched the hay rake onto the John Deere tractor, clambered aboard, and headed out to the farm, the bills of their seed caps yanked down over their eyes. Half an hour later Ervin's mother stepped onto the porch and shuffled off towards the post office.

198

After she'd walked a block, I raced down the street and up the steps. Cicadas buzzed in the trees in their heavy sawing manner, scrambling my brain, reminding me how Ervin loved them.

I knocked, and heard the squeak of an easy chair, and the slow tread of footfalls nearing. The doorknob rattled. Ervin lifted the white lace curtain, and his face filled the small window. He grimaced and flung the curtain back. "Go away, Biddee!" his muffled voice said.

"Erv! I just want to talk. To say I'm sorry. Erv!" But he ignored me. I rapped on the green door until my knuckles were red and sore. The cicadas fell into silence. The weight of the day stuck to my skin. Neighbors' eyes bored into my back. I knocked again. Nothing.

What had I expected?

For several days as I made my way to the post office to get my newspapers, I stood in the cool shadows of the trees down the street for a moment, gazing at Ervin's house. The sun blazed, the wind creaked the trees, the rain plopped around me. I watched the family come and go through their green door. They paid me no more attention than farmers did barn cats.

In the evening the yellow lights streamed through the cream-colored shades, blinking on and off. Sometimes the door opened, and Ervin shuffled onto the porch, his head pointed heavenward as if he was going to howl. I wanted to whisper his name, but the lump in my throat stopped all words. Later I heard lugubrious notes from the foot organ in the attic of the garage, and I knew he was playing again.

Summer drifted toward fall, and loneliness and I linked hands. The friendship between Ervin and me was as dry and dead as the early-summer flowers. I had failed him.

Nobody else shared my love of nature like Ervin did (of cicadas' humming he said, "Ooh, like a bee buzzing in my ear"); or music (Ervin played sad pop tunes on the foot organ in their garage loft while we sang); and baseball, the N. Y. Yankees for me, and the L.A. Dodgers for Ervin. I was alone.

199

At first I cursed the other guys for drawing me into their plot. But as days grew shorter, and the ache greater, I realized I was angriest with myself for lacking courage.

How could I expect Ervin to cherish my friendship if I ignored his feelings, his humanness? I shook my head in dismay.

I still played baseball, but in a halfhearted, sad way. I was living in a sea of molasses.

Evenings began to cool. Ducks and geese turned their longing looks south. The music of frogs and crickets was short and shivery. School began. I wouldn't see Ervin there in school during the winter. It would seem like he, too, had gone south. But did it matter now?

One cool fall Saturday a few of us were set to meet at the diamond to play what could be our last game of the season, as snow had already fallen twice, and barely melted. I went early. As I passed Ervin's silent house, I gazed longingly at the door. Should I knock? No. No use piling up more rejection. I bowed my head and walked by.

A block later at the edge of the fading outfield grass of our stadium, I spotted the remnants of what had been a scraggly yellow flower. I knelt to pick it, and seconds later, sensed a presence.

"It's-it's almost dead, isn't it, Biddee?" Like our friendship? I looked up at Ervin, smacking a ball into his mitt. "Hi, B-B-Biddee," he stammered, strings of saliva glinting.

Slowly he raised his index finger, and as tears filled my eyes, I raised mine in return.

"Do-do you think I could watch baseball today?" he said, as though he had been the culprit who had wronged me.

"Oh Ervin," I said. "Of course you can..."

By now other players were gathering around home plate. Someone leaped in the air, swinging a bat downward, mimicking Ervin's odd swing, laughing loudly. I gritted my teeth. Now was the chance to atone for my sins. But how?

Then an idea blossomed in my brain. "C'mon, Ervin."

"But B-B-Biddee..."

I led him towards home plate. The others looked nervous.

To decide who chose first, we threw a bat, as usual, grabbing the handle, fists on top of fists until I won, as I'd hoped. I could pick the best player, which practically guaranteed a victory, and they waited for me to do it.

I took a deep breath. In a strong voice, loud and clear, I said, "I'll take Ervin."

Perfect Summers Nevermore

Winter set in with its plunging temperatures that froze the hairs in my nose, and raging winds that clicked hard ice pellets against my parka hood, and whirled the surface of the deep snow into fantastic patterns.

At times during my paper route I detoured to Woehl Stadium. My heart was heavy as I viewed the dugout packed with snow, the backstop standing solitary in the cold, white drifts, and the bases invisible beneath the thick white carpet. I sighed.

When would summer come? When would we begin playing baseball in our stadium once more, and repeat last year's almost-perfect summer – except for the firecracker incident.

Finally the north winds quit blowing, and the air grew warmer. The water dripped and trickled over the land. The odors of spring filled the air, rotting plants, along with sweet smells of the flowers and tree blossoms. A patina of green began to cover the brown soil. Time to begin, to have fun once more, to play baseball at Woehl Stadium. Life would be perfect again.

So I thought. But reality was different. In a few short months the spell had been broken. Life had changed and baseball was no longer a priority for many players, who were working, on the farm, in their parents' gas station or implement dealership.

For a couple more years we played baseball at Woehl Stadium, but it had become a minor hobby instead of the main event. When I realized I was not the fearsome baseball player I'd thought I was, my interest in playing dwindled. Just like that, our perfect summers ended too.

Beastly Learning

Communing With Fish

One day my step-grandfather John Fetzer surprised Ron and me. He clapped me on the shoulder and said, "Yah, da Billy. '*Fisch*?" (Fish?)

I was starved for the attention of any man so the excursion with Grandpa Fetzer was more than welcome.

At Lake Hoskins, fifteen miles south of Wishek, he gave each of us a fishing pole he had fashioned, six feet of bamboo with a long black line attached to the end. It may have been crude, but I didn't know any better, and I was delighted.

He handed us each a red-and-white bobber, a small lead weight, and a black barbed hook to tie on the line. He showed us how to tie a knot so the fish wouldn't tear the hook loose. I was flabbergasted. Nobody had ever directly shown me how to do anything like that before – or really almost how to do anything.

Finally he showed us how to thread a squirmy wet earthworm onto the hook, and drop the entire setup over the bank and down into the water of Lake Hoskins.

We stood in the dry grass on the high bank and waited. He motioned for us to keep our eyes on the bobbers. Most of the red on the bobber was pulled down into the water by the weights on the line, so I watched the white. For a couple of minutes the bobbers lay motionless on the lake, the water so still the blue sky and white clouds seemed painted on the surface.

Then one by one our bobbers quivered, sending out miniature waves, then dropped under and popped back up.

Ron yanked his pole, jerking the line out of the water, with no fish. And no worm. He groaned in disappointment.

Sitting in an old chair, wearing his peasant hat and suit coat, Grandpa shook his head at Ron. Then Grandpa saw his own bobber go under and stay down. He pulled the line tight, and with both hands jerked the bamboo pole up, setting the hook in the fish's mouth. Keeping the line taut, he wound the black string around the bamboo pole until the bobber appeared, followed by the weight, and a hideous-looking bullhead, the first I'd ever seen. Grandpa removed the fish from the hook and dropped it onto the grass, where it flopped back and forth.

Soon my bobber dipped and stayed under, and I felt the pressure of the unseen fish on the other end. After a moment, I yanked the pole with both hands, as Grandpa had done. The fish jerked back, and I felt its weight and strength. I stepped back, and pulled the line out from the water, the bobber and weights following, and at the end, a nice shiny wriggling five-inch perch came up and flopped on the grass.

It was my first time fishing, and the first fish I'd ever hooked – and I was hooked too.

After we'd caught a few more perch and bullheads, we put the fish in a water-filled pail with a cover, and drove silently home, Grandpa in his German thoughts, we in our English.

He never took us fishing again. We discovered that he had taken us as a favor for Grandma, who had babysat us for the first time that day when mom was working in the voting booth, and Grandma was overwhelmed. Afterwards when Grandma was asked how babysitting us had gone, she said, "I'd rather watch a herd of wild horses."

That winter my great-uncle Leaman Boschee took me out fishing in his hut, one of dozens arrayed atop the ice in different areas on a local lake. Cars and pickups were parked next to the fishing huts. Holy mackerel! Could the ice support that much weight? Even inside Leaman's fishing place I stepped gingerly.

Each corner contained a trap door that opened to reveal the ice beneath. Leaman used an ice auger to cut a large round hole in the ice, creating an opening so I could peer down and watch fish swim effortlessly back and forth in the cold clear water.

I baited my hook and dropped the line into the water. A few minutes later I held my breath as a foot-long fish swam right up to the bait, opened its mouth, and gulped it down.

I yelled. I jerked the fishing rod but forgot to use the reel. I pulled the wet freezing line out of the water by hand.

As I strained with the line, feeling the fighting weight of the fish on the end and icy water dribbling down my arm, a long lean fish rose up out of the water, wriggling like mad, smattering drops of water in all directions. The fish dangled a few inches above the hole.

"Hey, a northern pike!" Leaman shouted.

I stood, mouth agape, admiring the beauty of my silvery catch. But I didn't react swiftly enough. With a sudden wrench the beautiful yellowish white-spotted fish snapped its body. Now the line suddenly felt light as air. The pike broke loose, dropped back into the water, circled the hole and angled its nose down into the deeps. Leaman, on his knees beside me, flashed his hands down into the frigid water. He seized the fish and scooped it out onto the floor where it lay thrashing. He wiped his hands on his pants, stood, opened the door and pitched the pike through a heavy fog of air out onto the ice, where it froze. Later he filleted it, and we shared it half and half.

He never took me fishing again either. Perhaps because Mom had married Walter, and Leaman, with children of his own, figured taking a boy fishing was a father's job. But I'd caught the fever, so I fished whenever I could, feeling like an adult, even providing occasional food for our table.

Fishing Lines

By the time I was eleven, I had fallen in love with fishing – hook, line and sinker, summer or winter, morning, afternoon or evening. But my wheels, a bicycle, limited chances to angle because of the six plus miles to the lakes.

One day my fervor led me to Red Lake, eight miles, for perch and bullheads – and maybe a northern pike. I stood on the shore and cast, to the pleasant zingggg as the bobber, weights, and hook zoomed out and splashed down.

A minute later my bobber dunked half-heartedly, and I pulled in a three-inch bullhead. Too small. Tossed it back in. After several lost worms, I moved down the shoreline hoping for better luck.

Fifty feet farther along the bank my luck changed. Within ten minutes my bobber stayed down. I waited a second, then jerked the rod to set the hook. The fish tried to swim away, and bent the rod a few inches, but I reeled in an ugly black bullhead with a yellow belly. Eight inches long. My smile grew ear to ear. I grabbed its wet smooth body, avoiding the barbs on its fins that could inflict a painful sting, as well I knew. I wondered for a moment if these fish used their fin stingers as weapons against their enemies. It seemed logical.

I removed the hook, slid the stringer chain through the gills, and returned the stringer back into the lake to keep the fish alive. No catch and release. Fish were to eat.

During the next hour I caught five bullheads and one perch, all of edible size. Then the biting stopped closer to shore. So I flung my line out further with a more powerful sharp flick of the wrist. The reel sang and I watched the hook, covered brown by a wriggling worm, the gray weights, and the red-and-white bobber all fly away and splash into the water. Along with a silver strip that glinted in the sunshine and plopped into the lake, raising a spume of spray.

Unknown for but a second. I glanced at my wrist. Oh no! Only a band of untanned white remained.

That watch was a precious jewel. For the few weeks I'd had it I felt like an adult it. I had earned it by signing new customers for my paper route, but had broken the metal band and not repaired it properly. Now it was gone. I swore.

The middle-aged man casting from the shore nearby, asked what was wrong. I wanted to cry. I tapped my wrist.

"That's what it was?" he said. "I saw it and wondered. It didn't go far. You could wade out and get it. The lake isn't deep here. Not even to your waist."

I couldn't swim, and was afraid of water, so I felt relieved I might be able to retrieve my watch, as the stranger said. I believed him; why wouldn't I?

I reeled in my line so I wouldn't get tangled in it, laid the rod and reel down, and sat on the ground. I took off my socks and shoes, figuring I could feel the watch with my toes, removed my pants to the man's mirth, and walked down in my undies and waded in.

And plummeted straight down into cold suffocating water over my head. The frigidity caused me to inhale. No more thoughts of a watch. Just survival. Thought I was going to drown. Kicked my legs and flailed my arms as hard as I could. Popped to the surface, coughing and gasping. Grabbed a mouthful of air. Sank back under. Kicked to the surface once more, somehow closer to shore. Floundered to the bank, and lay half in and half out, expecting some help. Which didn't come.

My advisor laughed. "Never seen such a surprised look!" He laughed again. I considered imbedding a fishhook in his genitals, twisting it and laughing.

I dressed, grabbed my stringer of fish from the lake, and mounted my bike. He said, "Don't be mad." Ha!

I biked eight miles home, distressed the entire way at the man's duplicity – and my buying into it.

Before, fishing had been fun, and provided healthy eating for the family. Afterwards, for a while at lakes, especially Red Lake, I was afraid, remembering that cold water, thinking I'd drown. Should have finished swimming lessons.

Spider Lessons

One morning I spotted a spider web large as a washtub glittering with dew in the early sun. It was frail as an illusion, the web attached to the rabbit cage on one side and the chicken coop on the other. Could it snare an unwary chicken? I slipped that idea into my back pocket in case we ever lost one of the silly birds that Ron and I were supposed to watch.

When I studied the web, I was amazed by its symmetry, a beautifully-constructed work of art. The spider crouched in the center of the web.

I was mystified. How did the creature know which wriggles meant prey, and which didn't? Racing back and forth and up and down the web with every twitch, attempting to see which was a meal and which was, say, the brush of a breeze, the tap of a raindrop, the touch of a feather, or seed, the plonk of a leaf, or a bit of dirt, would kill the spider of exhaustion first. Or starvation.

And how did the spider know which wriggle meant edible food, like the difference between a fat mosquito or gnat instead of a wasp, so it could slide down on a gossamer strand, sting, and eat lunch, or wrap it in white strands for supper or breakfast the next morning?

I tapped a strand with my finger. The spider arched its legs, but didn't move. Hmm. Poked a twig on a strand. No reaction. Dropped a leaf on it. Nothing. I frowned. Did the spider recognize dozens, even hundreds of different vibrations that weren't food?

Seemed too complicated. But nature... I clapped a fly, but killed it. And two more. I wounded the next one, and dropped it on the web where it buzzed, struggling.

The spider recognized new food, racing down towards the fly, its six eerie eyes glittering above its poison-mouth parts. The fly frantically revved its torn wings and wiggled its hairy legs.

Darting in, the spider stung the fly. Once. Twice. After a while the movement of the fly grew weaker and weaker. When it stopped struggling, the spider wrapped it with white wisps spewed out of its spinnerets.

Aha! I figured the spider must recognize prey because it kept moving, like the fly, fighting to escape the web. No leaf, or wind, or finger would do that. I'd bet a harsh wiggle meant a large prey, perhaps dangerous to the spider, so it could beware the summons, or ignore the jiggling, if it chose.

After watching the fly disappear into a white coffin, I had second thoughts. Sometimes in my life I felt like the fly, trapped in a large strong web not of my own making. With a twig I poked the spider away, grabbed the partially-mummified fly, and with difficulty unwrapped a few filaments.

Too late. The fly was dead. I dropped it back on the web, and climbed up onto the roof of the chicken coop, lying on the shingles and gazing up into the partly cloudy sky, feeling sorry for myself. And for the fly.

Minnow Pond Adventures

One summer afternoon I walked to the railroad tracks on my way to the minnow pond. Tied to the belt loops of my jeans were the handles of two one-gallon Karo syrup pails.

I'd left before being fingered for more chores, fleeing the glow of radiant light of work-yet-to-be-done gleaming in my parents' eyes, shining on me: a long litany of labor. If I was absent, they couldn't squeeze me.

My threadbare gray slacks were old, unsightly and stained, but the big pockets allowed me to cart treasures that caught my eye. A dead cicada, prairie rose petals, old penny, colored glass, a rusty nail, a jack-knife with one good blade.

I had punched the bottom of one pail full of two-penny nail holes. The pails bonged against my thighs as I kicked rocks, listening to them clatter on the gravel road. Each bong of the pails rang out "freedom," and moved me one step farther away from the demands of work at home.

Jack Hellerud, the depot agent, stood on the platform loading milk barrels, and when he saw me, he stopped and studied my progress down the road. When I stepped into the tracks, he pointed at his watch and yelled something that I couldn't hear. I waved and walked to my exciting new world.

The Soo Line Depot near an elevator in Wishek.

Walking on the tracks instead of biking through town (where Walter might catch me and present me with work) increased the distance to two miles one way, but I didn't care. I felt emancipated.

As I walked I made a game where each footstep had to land on a railroad tie, then changed to each step had to miss a tie. Then I walked outside the rails on the dirt that slanted down to the water-filled ditches, bulging from recent heavy rains.

Water frightened me. I couldn't swim, and feared the water in the ditches, part of the marshes. The water was black and terrifying, certainly deep enough to drown me. I shuddered.

I avoided the *Brenveed* (burnweed) because I'd hear a single touch would sting harshly. As the sun grew hotter, the sharp smell of creosote rose off the ties.

I balanced on a rail, arms outspread, to see how far I could walk. Only a dozen shaky steps in squeaking shoes until I fell off. Rubber bands around the toeboxes affected my steps, and my soles were smooth and slippery. But the games were fun, and I was free.

Nothing else mattered because I was out in the nature that I loved, the nature that renewed me, the nature that made no demands of me, except that I glory in it.

My wild companions surrounded me. Meadowlarks cried "tea-CHER lost HER pet-EE-coat," yellow-headed blackbirds made their deep galunk calls, American bitterns sounded like they were dropping large rocks in the water, blackbirds with red slashes on their shoulders swayed on flimsy ends of reeds seemingly incapable of holding them, chirping "Whoo reee, whoo ree!" Mallard males with the shiny green head quack-quacked a welcome.

Frogs in the sloughs peeped and croaked, crickets chirped, gophers in fields squeaked, butterflies created orange watercolors in the air, and flying grasshoppers buzzed back and forth in front of me, the undersides of their brown wings flashing crimson. I loved this massive cageless zoo.

211

The summer heat created a shimmering film wavering the landscape, as though a giant hand had ruffled it. My cup overflowed.

As I walked, sunlight flared off the burnished rails ahead of me. A half-hour later, pressed forward by the sun's warm arm around my shoulders, I spotted the flash of water. I raced ahead, pails thumping like drums against my thighs.

With a great sigh I slid halfway down the bank of the thirty-foot-long pond. A minnow-laced stream moved slowly through the water, and lapped high on the banks.

This innocent place was also a wild, lawless place, sometimes savage and cruel, as nature can be. I untied the pails and set them aside. My movements startled the minnows to retreat into the deeps of the pond, becoming tiny ghostly figures five feet down near the bottom. I did not move. Moments later, curiosity drew them slowly up towards the surface one by one until a hundred crowded together in a dense school of myriad sizes and colors, hovering, slender tails wriggling in place as they studied me with pinprick eyes.

Suddenly I yelled and sprang at them. They exploded in every direction like glass shattered into myriad pieces when dropped on cement. I chuckled.

I was intrigued. How could a mass like that careen helter-skelter in every direction at hundreds of miles per hour without a single accident during their furious flight? Not a one turned wrong or braked late. None smacked headlong into each other, or crashed into the bank, leaving a carnage of little fish bodies, bloodied and broken, a massive wreck on the underwater autobahn. A miracle.

I retrieved a length of white clothesline from my pocket, and tied it securely to the handle of the pail with holes in the bottom. I wound the other end of the line about my palm, and flung the pail to the center of the brown-tinted water. I smelled cow dung, skunk, a dead animal decaying, new-cut hay, all wafting on a gentle breeze that ruffled my hair and dried my sweaty brows. The rope slid roughly through my palm until I closed my fingers and stopped it.

The pail thunked holes-down, and the minnows darted away like shot arrows. After a minute, the pail listed and water gushed over the lip. A minute later it sank, growing dimmer and dimmer.

When it struck the bottom, trailing its umbilical cord, tendrils of mud obscured the Karo lettering. The pail lay at an angle with the open mouth a few inches above the bed of the pond. A group of minnows swam near the opening to check this new intruder into their domain, darting back and forth until a single brave one hovered near the opening, twitched, and entered. Others followed. I gripped the line and waited until a few more stragglers drifted into the trap.

I jerked the clothesline, lifting the pail off the bottom, drawing the cold wet rope in hand over hand, the pressure of the water within the pail pinning the minnows inside. I clunked the pail, gushing streams of water through the nail holes, on the bank, filled the other one with pond water, and peered at my bounty, a dozen fishes an inch to two long, flitting frantically to and fro in their diminishing wet world. Before they could slice themselves on the aluminum curls, I poured them into the full pail in a series of plops, blips of energy that speeded around and around the pail.

"Beautiful!" I said, watching them.

I chose one minnow – not a stickleback, whose name tells all that needs to be known of it – pinned the minnow with my palm against the side of the can and pulled the little fish out. As I held it, I was shocked once more by the raw strength of the wriggling little body throbbing with life as it whipped its tail and head back and forth, trying to escape.

I studied its precise beautiful tail, tiny scales, and the visible lateral line which provided its balance, which helped it discover prey or avoid enemies. I studied the gaping blood-red gills as they opened and closed, losing color with each gasp, until I feared it would die. I dropped it back into the pail where it skittered away.

Minnows fascinated me, silver, gold, brown, and black shards of flesh that darted every direction, like tiny colored

213

arrows. At first, all minnows looked alike. Until you looked closer.

Yellow-gold carp minnows were the prettiest, with a dorsal fin along half its backbone; chubs sported flakes of gold in their fins with light purple below their lateral line; the gold-green-finned shiner and the fathead with its silver belly and dark lateral lines were as distinct from each other as my brothers and me.

Despite the beauty and small size of minnows, some proved dangerous, their dorsal fins sharp weapons. The first time a stickleback jammed five dorsal spines into my hand, I clutched my stinging fingers for hours, and never made that mistake again.

I lay and closed my eyes, chewing grass, rubbing a finger lightly over my eyeballs to see the fantastic colors the sunlight made. I was content. What could go wrong?

Later I tossed the catch-pail into the water again. Some minnows had not noticed their missing friends, or their curiosity got the best of them, and swam into the pail. I pulled the pail in and nabbed ten more, pouring them in with their mates. Enough bait for an afternoon of fishing for bullheads and perch at Green Lake.

Time to leave. I tied the empty catch-pail back onto my belt loop. Water from it dripped on my thigh as I picked up the pail with the minnows and water. I climbed up the bank onto the railroad tracks and began walking back toward home. If I walked slowly, maybe I would miss some chores.

Near-Disaster on the Tracks

As I walked on the ties, I noticed once more that the ditches were brimful with water. My eyes kept drifting over to the deep dark pools. I shuddered.

I smiled. No need to worry. I kept walking, hearing the empty pail bong every other step. I wondered if I had time to stop at the rock piles at Wishek Concrete and Lumber Products Co. and search for agates.

I shook my head. The water in the minnow pail would get too warm and the fish would die. I switched the heavy pail to my other hand, and touched the rail with my foot.

And felt it come alive. Mentally I saw Jack Hellerud point at his watch. Suddenly I knew what he meant.

A moment later behind me a train whistle shrieked, "Getttt offfff! Getttt offfff! Getttt offfff!"

I turned. The train was half a mile away, an engine pulling dozens of dark maroon cars moving in what appeared to be slow motion around a curve. The light at the front of the engine burned yellow. I felt the vibrations increase. Amid the thumping of my heart.

Big trouble. Figured maybe forty seconds away.

Couldn't outrun it. Glanced at the deep water. No.

Couldn't stand outside the tracks either to let it pass. One time I stood too close to a rushing semi and got sucked towards it. The bigger train would yank me under the wheels. Grind me up.

Lie between the tracks while the train roared over me? I'd crawled under boxcars. But the cow catcher would crunch me.

I turned and looked at the water again. The ditches were full as far ahead as I could see. No safe place.

Except the highway, where it crossed the tracks. By the minnow pond. Where I'd come from. Maybe two blocks. Back toward the train, the pounding pounding train. A third of a mile away. Coming fast.

215

No choice. I had to run. Toward the train. The highway seemed a mile away. The earth quaked.

The train thumped and roared and throbbed. Growing larger. Nearer. The whistle shrieked and shrieked and shrieked.

I flung the pail of minnows into the water. The catch-pail bonged and bonged against my thigh. I ran. Raced. The ties shuddered.

A rubber band snapped. My sole flopped. Inanely I wanted to stop and fix it.

My heart hammered. The whistle shrieked. The ground shuddered. I pissed my pants. Warm and wet.

I raced frantically. The beast loomed ever larger. If I fell, the great steel beast would pulverize me down and under. It screamed. Me too.

The train loomed, the horn blaring, blaring. Too close! I squeezed my eyes shut. I dove to the left. The world was thunder. A whipping hurricane of air tore at me. I struck the pavement, and rolled. The pail bonged. Wind ripped at my clothes. Stars danced behind my closed eyes. The monster thundered by.

Hardly able to speak I yelled faintly, "I made it," and louder, "I made it!"

Peering at the train moving down the tracks, I saw the engineer poke his head out. Shook his fist at me. Trembling, I sat up. My palms burned where I'd torn open the skin. Blood. But it was still pulsing through my veins.

I stood and shakily began walking toward home. On the highway. I might catch heck for avoiding work, but I'd had a glorious afternoon, escaped death, and on balance, it was a grand day.

Rabbit Meat

One time Grandpa Fetzer asked me to help butcher our full-grown rabbits. I was overjoyed to get special attention from a man, even at twelve years old.

He smiled and clapped me on the shoulder, and said, "Yah, da Billy!" In our backyard he pointed at the rabbit hutch and said, "*Geps mir haasa.*" (Give me the rabbits.) I was used to butchering, so I knew the process with Grandpa would be fun.

I crawled into the hutch, grabbed a big gray rabbit and pulled it out, struggling and fighting, and took it into the chicken coop to Grandpa. He grabbed it by its ears, and unceremoniously cracked a foot-long board sharply against the back of the rabbit's neck. I heard the spine snap. The rabbit jerked and went limp.

Grandpa tied the back legs on a rafter, and tested the edge of a knife with his thumb. "Yah," he said, looking at me and smiling.

He cut off the front legs, sliced the furry skin open, and yanked the pelt down, exposing the pink ribs and dark entrails. One more jerk and the entire skin came loose, with surprisingly little blood. He divided the body, removed the entrails and dropped them in a bucket, separating choice parts, like the heart and liver.

When I brought him the seventh and last rabbit, Grandpa handed me the two-by-four and motioned that I should hit the rabbit. "*Du,*" he said, "*Schlog.*" (You hit.)

My eyes must have bugged big as softballs. I didn't mind killing insects up close, or bigger animals with a rifle from afar, or watching Grandpa dispatch them. But peering into the eyes of the rabbit and seeing the life force I was going to end, seemed too much. But I didn't want to disappoint Grandpa.

So I took a deep breath, grabbed the two-by-four, rough and heavy in my hand, and whacked the rabbit hard on the back of the neck. Nothing happened. Except the rabbit squirmed mightily. I rapped him again, and again, and again, harder each time, until his body finally went limp. Grandpa smiled at me, a bit strained.

We hung it from the rafter, and Grandpa handed me the knife, and showed me where to begin. After cutting off the front legs and slicing the hide loose, while he said, "*Vorshtig, vorshtig,*" (Careful, careful,) I grabbed the fur, and began to strip it down.

Halfway finished, a high piercing squeal erupted as the rabbit came awake, jumping and squirming. I was skinning it alive!

Grandpa grabbed the board and whacked the rabbit so I heard the spine break, and the rabbit went limp. He rapped it once more for good measure. At that moment I decided I would never butcher rabbits again.

For days in my mind I heard the terrible squeal of the rabbit, and I began to wonder about killing birds and gophers and insects.

Sunbathing Chickens

Of all the works foisted on us, the vilest plot to steal our childhood happiness was baby-sitting the chickens. Shade did not appear until late afternoon, and none in a place where we could glory in it and still watch the chickens, so we were forced to sit on the ground in the broiling summer sun. We hated it, surrounded all afternoon by fifty-five-gallon barrels of boredom.

That day in the back yard near the chicken coop, Ron and I were repairing our baseball tools, tightening the rawhide on the pockets of our baseball mitts and spitting in the pockets, pounding brads into the handle of a splintered bat, and restringing the seams of a worn-smooth cowhide ball so we could play baseball. That's when we heard the distinctive rumble of our stepdad's 1956 IHC pickup starting behind Sayler Brothers Hardware two blocks away where he worked.

Uh oh. Our freedom teetered on the fence of jeopardy. Either Walter was driving to a job laying carpet and installing tile in a house somewhere in town, or coming home to corral us for some kind of work – or both. Helping with his store-sponsored work, or hoeing potatoes, picking bugs, washing windows, the list was endless. All to make sure we did not have any fun. Including the worst job in the world: watching our chickens so they didn't escape.

We perked up our ears, and when the pickup rattled closer, we scrambled up on top of the chicken coop and laid flat on our backs, feeling the rough wooden shingles scrape against the back of our head and elbows and hands. Sparrows chirped cheerily above us in the thick greenery. Of course they didn't have to go to work if we were caught.

We held our breath, as the vehicle's tires crunched gravel in the alley a dozen feet away. The blue of his pickup flashed through the leaves as it motored by.

But we were safe. He'd never found us before. And he wouldn't today. We'd spread-eagle here watching the birds until Walter gave up. He had sniffed out every other hiding spot – basement bedroom, furnace room, boxcars, pigweed forest, ravine, ball diamond, pigweed – but he'd never stumbled onto this fortress, shrouded by the thick leaves of elm and box elder trees concealing us, making us impeccably safe.

A moment later his pickup, lurching back and forth to avoid alley potholes, turned the corner onto the street along our back yard. Walter parked, the door slammed, and his shoes scraped the macadam.

Silence for a moment. Half a minute later the door to the chicken coop three feet below us creaked open. I frowned. Why would he go there?

The door closed, and when I heard his voice, a pit formed in my stomach. "Billy and Ronnie!" he yelled, "Get down off that roof. I know you're up there. There's work to be done!"

I was pinned to the shingles by the weight of surprise. "How does he know we're here?" I hissed.

"I dunno," Ron whispered. "Maybe he's just guessing."

Walter had stepped off to the side of the coop beneath some of the leaves where he was no longer guessing: he could see us. "Get down here. Now."

I swore as we clambered down. "He always knows. He always figures it out."

Our executioner meted out the sentence: another day on the rack. "Watch the chickens today. Both of you. And you'd better make sure none of them get away. Or *baus oof.*" (Look out.) Inwardly I groaned. He said, "No reading. Just watching the chickens. I shouldn't have to say if any get out, catch them!"

In school, neighbor kids said that the summer before, they'd had the good fortune to catch four wild chickens. "Really wild ones," one boy said. "But we grabbed them, and our mom cooked them up good. Yum Yum." Coincidentally, Walter noticed we were missing four chickens that summer.

220

So zero fun. No baseball. No fossil hunting on the rock pile at Wishek Concrete. No bike riding. No digging in the ravine. Only staring at those ditzy white chickens.

"And put your baseball stuff by the door away!"

I slapped my forehead. No wonder! That's how we got tripped up! Dang! And another hiding place lost!

After talking to Mom in the house, Walter drove away. Despite chicken duty, I was grateful I didn't have to work with him on a carpet job, which entailed occasionally handing him tools. Boring! At least here we could talk with each other.

A half-hour later my friend Tom drove past on his bike, and saw us lying on the ground. He pushed his bike up the hill onto our yard, and sat down beside me.

"What are you doing?"

"Watching the chickens, I said.

"I know that. But why?"

I sighed. "So they don't get out of the fence."

He looked at the fence with a frown. "I don't see any holes in it."

"No, they fly over the fence."

"Why not just build a higher fence?"

I shrugged. "The old man doesn't want us to have any fun. He just wants us to work all the time, like him."

The sun's rays were relentless. Sweat burned as it dribbled into my eyes.

Tom said, "Your old man wouldn't know if we left."

"Yes he would," I said. "He'd know."

Ron added. "He always knows."

"How?" Tom said. He picked a stalk of grass and clipped it between his teeth. So did I.

I shrugged. "Spies? X-ray vision? Who knows."

As though mocking us, the chickens pecked up goodies in the small sunlit area, and then retreated into shade created by the chicken coop in the trees behind it. Shade we didn't have.

"Why not watch from the roof?" Tom indicated with his chin. "At least there's shade there."

I shook my head. "Can't see all of the fence. Chickens might get out and we couldn't see them when they ran away. So no dice."

Boredom set in like a stifling blanket. Tom began shooting at the chickens with an imaginary rifle. We followed, hoping the beasts might somehow keel over so we could go exploring.

When that shooting flagged, I picked up a couple of rocks and began to whip them at the chickens, just to startle them. Most missed. But one brained our rooster right in the head. He dropped like a bag of white sand.

"Oh God, you killed him!" Ron wailed.

"Oh shit," I said. Time stood still. "We're dead!"

I rushed to the fence. The rooster lay unmoving. What could we do? Bury him? Or say he got caught in the big spider web, and got eaten? Or escaped? Arrgh. No matter what, we were dead.

Then I had another idea. What if we laid him on the floor inside the chicken coop, like he'd just died! Chickens do die. Walter might be suspicious, but that just might work!

I grasped the gate to enter and grab the body. But just then the rooster wriggled, his legs flailing, and stirred. He stumbled to his feet and stood unsteadily. He croaked a bizarre, other-worldly sound, twisting around and around in a stunned waltz of confusion.

"He's alive!" Ron said.

"Woof!" I said, limp. "That was a close one."

Freed from our fears, we laughed, watching the rooster's curious action, staggering, like it was drunk. Would beer get chickens drunk? That would be weird. Even fun. But Mom was home, and Tom's dad, so we couldn't steal beer.

Still chuckling at the rooster's antics, and not having learned my lesson, I flung more rocks, hoping for a repeat. Soon we all threw rocks, scattering the chickens into noisy nervous knots, and thumping an occasional bird.

"Wait!" I said after a while, "Stop! The rocks! Walter will see them! We have to pick them up."

"Oh shit," Tom said.

"Unfortunately," I added.

We entered the yard, which smelled powerfully of ammonia. Manured our fingers picking up rocks. Stepped in some too.

Even with Tom around, boredom dragged on. With the chickens the source of our boredom, they were the source of our ire. We sought some way to irritate them. We tossed pebbles, but they were too small for the chickens to even notice. More boredom.

How about shooting pebbles with slingshots? But Walter would probably see them too. And I didn't want to root around in the manure again with my hands. We needed something smaller.

Then I had a brainstorm. "Better yet," I cried. "BBs! He'll never see BBs. I just got a new pack of 500." Our eyes gleamed. Tom biked home for his slingshot. Open season on chickens commenced. Swish thwap. Swish thwap. Swish thwap.

We shot and they jumped and squawked, and each time I felt vindicated for being forced to sit out in the hot sun to watch them. No matter where we hit the chickens, wings, rear, legs, we howled. We held our sides, which hurt from laughing.

We didn't notice that, one by one, the chickens were sitting down and staying down. A half hour later, as the temperature continued to climb, they all sat, their wings spread wide, sunbathing like so many kids at the swimming pool.

I was disappointed. They sure knew how to ruin a good time. A little bell should have tinkled in the back of my head. But it didn't.

When Walter came home for lunch at noon, he waved at Tom, just leaving for home on his bike. Walter headed toward the house, and then stopped, looking at the chickens, the overhead sun, the chickens again.

"What's wrong with the chickens?" He asked.

"Wrong with them?" Mom said.

"Never seen anything like it. All lying in the hot sun." He looked at us. "All right," he said ominously. "What did you do to the chickens?"

"Nothing," I said. "They're just, just, sunbathing."

"Sunbathing, my foot," he said. "Come with me."

He strode from chicken to chicken, his neck growing red, muscles in his temples pulsing. He wheeled. "Their legs are broken. All my chickens. And some are dead from sunstroke! Hook up the hoses! Hurry! We can probably save some of them."

We sprayed cold water on them until they were drenched, and then carried them into the shade.

After we were finished, Walter remained furious, and grabbed my arm. "This is for shooting the chickens," he said, whacking my fanny until it burned hot as the sun. "And this is for lying to me." More whacks. "And for not understanding that chickens are dumb animals. You protect dumb animals. You don't hurt them. Understand?" He shook me. "Six of them are dead. Others still might die."

After Ron's turn, Walter went to Tom's house and spanked him too.

Our family was forced to butcher all one hundred of those chickens weeks before normal, losing precious winter meat, because we'd forced them to "sunbathe" in that hot Dakota sun.

Blackbird Ethics

Beneath the blistering Dakota sun the day was growing ever more sweltering. My brother Ron and I had been banished by our stepdad to watch the few remaining scraggly chickens to see that they didn't escape. Who would have known that the hundred or so we'd shot with our slingshots a few weeks earlier would then have to be butchered? Well, the dead ones, yes. But...

I was twelve and had never been disciplined for killing anything before – gophers, mice, rats, grasshoppers, sparrows, or blackbirds – except for the frogs. We had maimed them.

So why the hullabaloo about chickens? Why were we getting punished for shooting those stupid birds?

Six had died of sunstroke, so I rationalized that we hadn't really killed any of them. The rest had been done away by family and relatives tossing dark looks our way because the chickens had to be butchered on a blistering summer day instead a cooler fall day. We were told they couldn't survive with broken legs. Who knew?

I shrugged. Seeing chickens get butchered was sweet revenge. No more prime time spent nursing them instead of playing baseball, hunting gophers, or searching for fossils. Ha! No chickens, no more watching.

Or so I thought. To my chagrin, a dozen more had been brought in from a farm, doubtless as punishment, so Ron and I were back watching them on a clear day with the hot yellow sun beating down on us, no books allowed. No playing baseball. No swatting down flying grasshoppers with pig weed and feeding the stunned insects to our cat. No slingshots. Nothing. Tom didn't seem willing to come over either. Could just as well have been handcuffed and manacled to the fence.

I was bored lying on the ground near the chicken fence as the temperature soared towards a hundred. I was startled out of my frustration by the sound of fluttering wings. I glanced up and saw a blackbird coast over the crown of a box elder tree, arch its wings, and glide down into what must have been the alluring and possibly cool black rectangle of the open chicken coop door.

We sprinted to the opening, scrambled inside, and slammed the door. Everything was black and hazy. Sweat trickled down my bare side, tickling, and my face was instantly wet. I wiped my eyes, peering through the gloom.

The smell of chicken manure, moldy grain, and mice assailed my nose, and white stars danced in my vision. When my eyes adjusted a moment later, I saw the blackbird perched on the top lath of the chicken roost five feet away, his wings outspread. He panted, his beak opening and closing around his sharp tongue.

One slow step at a time I moved closer, pausing when seeds crunched beneath my feet. But the bird seemed oblivious. Suddenly I snapped out my hand and nabbed him. He was warm, nestled in my palm. He barely struggled. Probably because of the heat. I had never held a live bird in my hand before – not counting chickens.

Ron threw the door open. In the light I was jolted to see a colorful red-winged blackbird. I blinked. "Oh, he's pretty," I said, stroking his head, and running my fingers through the brilliant red slash of feathers on his shoulders.

I examined the curve of his beak, the miniature nostrils, the small skull, gazed into the startling black eyes, fascinated by his eyelids that closed over his eyeballs like translucent lenses.

I studied the dark purple sheen of feathers, ran my fingers through the delicate down on his breast, and felt the exquisite toe knuckles, and his delicate claws at the end of his gray legs.

His life force throbbed warmly in my palm. Suddenly I felt dizzy with power. I could squeeze the bird until I stopped his shallow quick breathing, forever stilling the tiny heart hammering against my fingers. If I chose to.

I blew out my breath. His comeliness overwhelmed me and this required mental rearranging. I had never thought of a blackbird before as anything but evil. Disposable. "Better dead than alive." Certainly not lovely. As I studied the bird, I wasn't sure if red-winged blackbirds belonged to the class that ravaged farmer's crops. Its beauty overrode its evilness. Only one bird. I decided to spare it.

I prepared to open my hand. "We won't need..."

The bird clamped down viciously on the tender skin between my thumb and forefinger, drawing blood. I yelped and dropped him. He fluttered back into the darkness. I sucked my stinging wound.

I slammed the door so hard the grimy windows rattled. I raced back and forth after the fluttering bird, growing more and more frustrated. When I finally caught him, he bit me once more in the same spot. That changed my mind. I yelled, and finally clamped my fingers over his dangerous beak.

I sent Ron into the house for adhesive tape, an M80 firecracker that we called a depth charge, and matches. Luckily I wouldn't have to explain my momentary weakness to him.

When Ron returned we laid the thumb-sized red depth charge on the bird's chest, and wound white adhesive tape around his body to secure it. We left the fuse poking out.

"Serves him right, the little bastard," I said taking him outside, panting, like the blackbird. This was personal. I plucked a farmer's match out of the box, and scratched it against the white siding of the coop. The bird flinched, gazing at the flame with wide alarmed eyes. The plume of smoke seared my nostrils, and set my eyes watering. I touched the tip of the flame to the gray fuse. It hissed and spurted colored fire.

The bird struggled. I tossed it into the air. He flapped his strong wings, while I massaged my sore skin.

I suddenly hoped the fuse would fizzle, and the blackbird would power his way safely over the brown and green rooftops to his nest, where his wife would greet him effusively and three little chicks would peek out from behind her with their great bulgy eyes.

The bird did not get far. Blam! A powerful explosion shattered the silence, blowing the blackbird to smithereens. Guts sprayed every direction. A warm wet piece flopped onto my bare arm. As the echo died, a few black feathers hung suspended against the brilliant blue sky. They drifted down, the sole remnants of our dastardly deed.

Except for the guilt that haunted me for a long time from this articulation of our impotence and fury.

Torturing Animals

My cousin, one of our babysitters, showed us how to torture animals. He opened their rabbit cage and scrabbled around until he pulled one out by its ears. "This rabbit has been bad," he said. "It keeps digging out of the cage. It needs to be taught a lesson, taught not to do that."

He raised a hammer and thunked the rabbit solidly on the back of the skull several times until it quivered. "There. That should do it."

He smiled and patted the rabbit gently and placed it in the cage. A worm of discontent squirmed in my brain.

Another time he used a chunk of raw hamburger to entice a black dog to come to him. As the dog ate, my babysitter pulled a pepper shaker from his pocket, lifted the dog's rump onto his lap, raised its tail, unscrewed the cap, and poured half of the pepper onto the dog's anus. He rubbed it in, and put the dog down.

"Just watch," he said. Seconds later the dog's tail twitched. The dog groaned into the food. Suddenly it whined and nipped at its tail, and licked, and shook its head. My babysitter's eyes shone, and he chuckled.

I didn't know what to do. Whining piteously, the dog scrunched its butt on the sidewalk, leaving bloody streaks. The dog howled, *owooo owooo*, while my babysitter laughed. I felt bad for the dog and sick at heart.

The dog's heart-rending howl made me wonder if all animals, big and small – even grasshoppers – might also howl tiny unheard screams, like when I roasted them alive?

The final straw came the third time he babysat us. He brought out two wriggling gunnysacks from their garage. Out of one he brought a squalling cat, and tied string snugly around its chest just behind the front legs, which seemed to paralyze the animal. It blinked, but didn't move.

As he opened the other bag and lifted another cat out, which was hissing wildly, its claws scored deep scratches on his arm before he got the string tied around its chest. Cursing and daubing the blood on his arm with his handkerchief, he muttered that the little bastards were going to get what they deserved. Where had I recently said that?

He tied their tails together. He rubbed his hands on his thighs, and said, "All right. Now!" smiling a devilish grin.

He tossed the cats over a clothesline, one hanging on each side, touching each other. With a jackknife he cut the strings around their chests. The cats burst into life, hissing and screeching and writhing, their claws flashing as they raked the enemy causing them pain. Their legs blurred, their claws slicing and drawing blood and flinging tufts of fur into the air. They screeched, their sides soaking crimson. I shuddered, threw up, and ran.

"Billy! Come back. You'll miss the best part!"

By this time I was already an expert in dispensing death, killing vermin like mice, crop-eaters like blackbirds, and others, with BBs or .22 rifle. Most were clean kills.

Any predator that might disturb the stalks of the golden sea of wheat rising from the plowed fields around our community – or in the granaries – was in danger of execution. Because our town's welfare depended on healthy farm crops, we believed we were automatically absolved from the biblical sixth commandment of "Thou shalt not kill," for our perpetual killings.

But I was also cruel, the articulation of my impotence and anger in life. I used a magnifying glass to burn ants on the sidewalk, I roasted grasshoppers alive. Occasionally I felt bad, but not for the pain I inflicted on the poor little beasts – it was fun at the time, control and power to a kid who felt he had none. But I knew the torture was a sin, so I believed that my payback would be to spend eternity burning in hell, perhaps with a large cigarette lighter's flames focused on me, because I had burned those creatures. But hell was far in the future.

Now I reveled in the life-and-death power I held over the helpless animals. Grasshoppers bore the brunt of my cruelty, ostensibly because they spit on me, but I killed others of their ilk too. They hopped everywhere, so I developed a method to dispose of some of them for depredating the crops around town.

From an empty cinnamon tin I made a small griddle. My father's old cigarette lighter fit neatly under it. I cut a cinnamon tin in half, placed a grasshopper on the griddle, and quickly covered it with the half-tin. I flicked the flame alive on the cigarette lighter, put the flame underneath, and roasted the unfortunate creatures alive.

We thought the frantic pounding of the doomed grasshoppers was hilarious. I felt no remorse; only empowerment.

But watching my babysitter torture animals close-up changed my mind, convincing me that animals must never be mistreated. Yes, they had to be dispatched to protect crops, but no more cruelty.

Which meant no more roasting grasshoppers, or pulling them apart, or tearing off their wings, or cutting off the legs of frogs.

Personal Theater

The doe lifted her nose from the stream, her muzzle dripping water that glimmered like jewels in the sunlight. Though I had not moved, she had sensed me; perhaps my sudden intake of breath at her loveliness as she turned her head into the slanting beam of sunlight illuminating the glade.

She stared at me, drank again, and when I blinked, she turned and loped away, flinging diamonds of water into the air. At that moment I could never have enough of nature.

Two squirrels scampered up a tree, claws scratching the bark and tails flicking, while an owl observed the action with its wise-looking eyes and the wind twirled leaves gently.

Suddenly I realized my richness. Moneyed by gifts of nature – bumbling bees, screaming hawks, even the smell of the skunk, nature's eternal currencies.

I first comprehended the value of nature when I was ten, and peered around the prickly stems at the edge of the copse, searching for my brother, that day's enemy. Instead, on an expanse of sand I spotted our cat, crouched, tense, staring at the ground three feet ahead of her. Suddenly she sprang!

A flying grasshopper leaped up, a winged sliver of gold, but a quicker paw swatted it down, and the cat pounced. Seconds later, eyes half-closed in ecstasy, she clutched the morsel between her paws, nibbling and purring. Finished, she flashed a pink tongue over her paws and cast her eyes about as though to say "All right, where's my next bit of lunch?"

A fox running, a hawk diving, a mallard swimming. I shivered, awestruck at the stark allure of these dramas of nature, and the unforgettable images. They strummed a deep chord of joy inside me etched into my memory bank, images I could withdraw at any time and replay, hundreds over the years, my own personal theater, images that enriched me beyond imagining.

Gifts of images of nature can be deposited and then withdrawn, and withdrawn again. With interest.

Life and Death on the Plains

Growing up, life and death were our constant companions. One day our rabbit's pregnancy was announced when her long yellow teeth began tearing downy fur off her chest to line her nest. After that, I checked her nest every day, and caught her birthing six of her brood of fourteen babies.

She crouched, straddling while new hairless ones dropped out. She licked them, and they pushed their mouths into her fur, searching for food while mom birthed another.

Each baby seemed like a miracle. How did the mother know what to do? Or the babies? I shook my head in wonder.

Shortly a mass of little bodies squirmed around her, like big fat pink worms. She lay on her side and let them feed.

The babies intrigued me. So I crawled into the large outdoor cage and picked up the lovely little creatures one at a time and cuddled them, all warm and soft.

The next morning I was shocked to find two dead babies outside the nest. I blamed myself because I'd heard that handling newborns animals could cause parents to smell humans and reject them, but I'd played with them anyway.

Next I blamed predators. But found no burrowing holes into the cage. The door was solid. Only a snake could enter the pen through the small round spaces in the chicken wire. But snakes didn't lunch on prey or knock it on the head; they swallowed it whole.

When a third baby lay dead, I blamed the careless parents for trodding on the baby with their clodhoppers. I held funerals for the corpses, and buried the little ones in small graves near a baler in the machinery lot across the alley.

Later a farm friend said that rabbit parents sometimes killed their babies, and ate them, the father, feeling displaced, or the mother, overwhelmed or lacking enough food. I could hardly believe they would cannibalize their children.

From then on when the female acted pregnant, we removed the male. Problem solved.

Lack of Cultural Stories

Before I finally heard the history of the Germans from Russia, I might have concluded that nothing worthy had ever happened to my people, because the past was *verboten* (forbidden) and never discussed.

The opposite, I discovered was true. The history of the Germans from Russia was filled with unique occurrences, startling and unknown to me, because of the Great Silence of my people. After I left Wishek, I learned parts of our history.

In *Migration of Germans to Russia, The Colonists in Russia, and How They Left,* by Arthur Kramer, written in 1985, he said, "Two powerful impacts started the migration (from Germany.) The despair of the Seven Years War (1756-1763)... and utter poverty after the Seven Years War."

In 1763, amidst the darkness of forgotten centuries, Queen Catherine of Russia, herself German – Prussian – offered a Manifesto to entice Germans to migrate to the Russian Ukraine. The Manifesto read, in part, "We, Catherine the second, Empress and Autocrat of all the Russians at Moscow, Kiev, Vladimir ... We permit all foreigners to come into Our Empire, in order to settle in all the governments, just as each one may desire."

In exchange settlers received magnificent perks: free transportation to the settlement; no taxes for thirty years; interest-free loans for ten years; and forever, self-rule; religious freedom; and no military service for their children.

Within four years more than 6,000 families – 27,000 people, including my forebears – emigrated 1,500 miles to the Ukraine Volga. Each family received seventy-five acres, a wagon, plow, horses and tools, and sod houses.

As Kramer adds, "Of the Germans arriving in Russia, many were quite primitive. Only a few were farmers. The first wheat crop was eaten by gophers and grasshoppers."

Life was difficult. Crop failures were regular. Nomadic marauding tribes of Khirghiz, Kalmuka and

Bashkirs struck often, preying on hapless victims. Within ten years, 4,000 of the original Germans had lost their lives or been sold into slavery.

After the colonies blossomed over the next century, they became the agricultural pacesetters of Russia. But in 1871 Czar Alexander II decreed that "forever" meant one hundred years, and said: "One czar, one religion, one language!" nullifying all of Queen Catherine's Manifesto privileges, sending many Germans from Russia across the ocean in steerage to the United States, and some then to Wishek.

In 1932-33 Joseph Stalin's Terror Famine killed 3.9 million Germans in the Ukraine, including some of my relatives. Not one word of any of that unusual history was ever mentioned by my people. No stories.

Years later I discovered stories about hard times in hundreds of letters sent in the 1930s by Ukrainian Germans, and printed in German in many North Dakota newspapers, recounting the dire straits of those who remained behind:

The higher authorities have sent 150 men to our village, whose job it is to plague us half to death. At community gatherings the Commandants have told us, "Now that we have grown in power over you, you will see that wherever you destructive insects have settled in our land, that we have you in our hands, and know God will not drop manna from heaven to help you, and nowhere will anyone hear your miserable complaints. Hangings, shootings, starvation, and freezing – all of those will be done to you if you don't work to exactly meet the requirements of the predetermined Plan." But who can work? People are so weak that they fall over. They have ordered everyone from 13 to 100 years in age to work in the forests cutting trees and getting wood in the deepest snow, in the grimmest cold.

Dear brother, you write that you sent me five dollars. But I don't dare inquire if I have received, or might receive, the money. You shouldn't have sent it because now I am in much anxiety if they find out. When you write, send no money, otherwise I will end up deported. Sometime the sun again will shine on us.

Until May 6, the women remained in the monastery with the children, and after that date, were removed. But very few children went with, for some days 50 to 60 children died. I brought mine along with on the deportation, and though they became sick, none of them died. Our whole family is scattered. I am alone here among strange people.

We are so poor, just as our loving Savior, so that we don't know where to lay our heads. The place where we live has straw strewn on the earth, and pale walls in our room. There is one old bed cover that has been left behind, but no spoons, no plates, or anything else. No nothing.

We suffer so much, dear sister, that it can't be described. We ate sausage made of dead horse. We baked bread from potato peelings. I don't believe that we will be able to hold out much longer, so that we too will have to starve. Many have already starved. It would be best not to survive any longer, for all that we have already endured.

My dear sister, you know that to beg is not my manner. But there is no other way. Could you give each of my children a dollar? I beg you with my whole heart to help us. Otherwise we are lost. Goodbye. I'll see you again, I know, but not in this world, for my wish is in heaven. Yesterday, the sister of your son-in-law was arrested and sentenced to 20 years.

Perhaps the helplessness my people in Wishek felt in the face of the Terror Famine for their relatives and friends in the Ukraine during that era led to the town's unwillingness to look at the past, and increased the silence.

The Rest of the Stories

Nosebleed Plague

Grandma Fetzer added to my portends of doom each time she smashed open the kitchen door and thumped her Bible, reading verses predicting plagues from Revelation, the book that scared the bejesus out of me. I knew we didn't have bloody seas and rivers, scorching fire, dried-up rivers, and the torment of locusts stinging like scorpions – but other plagues?

According to Grandma Fetzer, humans who did not possess the sign of God on their forehead during the end time caught the plague, which sickened you and caused blood to spurt out of your orifices as you suffered and died in terrible pain. I checked my forehead to see if a mark was there, but it wasn't. Every sniffle or cough or sore throat heightened my fears, but nothing as badly as my spate of regular nosebleeds that ebbed and flowed. As they worsened, I believed I must have the plague.

"Am I going to die?" I asked Mom in desperation.

"From a nosebleed? Ach, don't be so dumb."

A cold washrag on my neck helped for a while. But the next day the blood poured out again. I was relieved to see that my other orifices weren't bleeding, so maybe my case of the plague wasn't fatal.

Or that I wasn't going to die right away. Still the nosebleed would not stop, and I knew you could die from loss of blood. "It must be the plague," I said. "Grandma said blood and plagues..."

"Ach, it's not the plague," Mom insisted, "it's just a nosebleed. It will stop."

But it didn't, so Mom called Dr. Gutowski for a home visit. Meant one thing: Deadly serious. I had the plague.

When I asked Dr. Gutowski how long it took for someone to die from the plague, he frowned and shook his head. "What plague? We fix nose." He produced what appeared to be a foot-long farmer's match with a dark head.

"I stick this up your nose," he said.

Yikes! How far? What if it stuck through my brain and came out the top of my skull? He grabbed my head and stuck the stick up my nose. He wiggled it around a couple of times until I had a powerful urge to sneeze. Instantly he yanked out the stick and I sneezed violently, spraying blood all over the floor.

After that the bleeding stopped. Gradually my fears of having the plague lessened. Still I wondered what would have happened if he hadn't pulled the stick out fast enough, and had his ministrations counteracted the Biblical plague?

Warm at Forty Below

Amidst the squeaking snow, the breeze raked my cheeks with its frigid fingernails as I hefted my bag over my shoulder, loaded with *Minneapolis Tribune* newspapers. Out delivering at 30° below zero exposed my parka-clad eleven-year-old body to wind that frisked me with those polar fingers, finding minor weak points in my clothing for momentary entry, a new spot each time I made a move, slipping on a snow-covered slab of ice, adjusting the heavy bag for comfort, or jerking when I was struck by a sudden blast of cold as I stepped into the open.

I'd been out for an hour, having finished half the paper route, and was uncomfortably cold. Nothing major. A nip on an earlobe here, a slice of wrist there, or the bottom of my neck when the weight of the newspapers pulled the parka zipper open an inch or two. Easily corrected. Unlike my frozen fingers flexing in my gloves, or my numb toes.

Meanwhile I tromped to my next customer, as far from home as I could get in my little city, amidst swirling tendrils of snow whirling around my ankles and snaking across the street, piling into pillows as though spun of silk and ice in the brick armory lot, marking the farthest edge of town.

I opened the door to toss in the next customer's paper when the inner door swung open. And I was attacked.

Or so it seemed. A hand grabbed the side of my parka hood and yanked me inside, a flood of warm air caressing my cheeks.

"You must be frozen," Chissie Ackerman said, "Poor thing!"

She lifted off my bag of newspapers, untied my hood, and unzipped my parka, removing it as the soothing balm of warm air wafted over me.

She yanked off my gloves and thrust a mug of steaming hot chocolate into my hands. I wrapped my fingers around it, glorying in the warmth. Heaven! The heady aroma nearly made me swoon.

Chissie pushed me down into an easy chair, muttering about torturing a handsome boy like me by sending him out into the Arctic cold. "To deliver newspapers, nonetheless."

She unbuckled my overshoes and pulled them off. Nothing remotely like this had ever happened to me before. But I wasn't going to fight it. I was putty in her hands.

She removed my shoes and set them on the floor, and tugged my socks off. While I sipped hot cocoa, she knelt, and gently began to rub circulation back into my frozen feet.

As she rubbed each toe and warmed my feet, she continued her patter about my being forced out in such weather. As she worked, I saw a Lincoln head penny collection book on a side table, and asked her about it. I was interested, but also was trying anything to stay in her warm house as long as I could with her massaging my feet.

"I collect Lincoln pennies," I said.

We commiserated about the holes in our collection that we had yet to fill, the rare and difficult to find 1909-S-VDB, 1914-D, 1922 plain, and 1931-S.

"Oh, I found a '31-S in change recently."

She raised her eyebrows. "Lucky you!"

"Found an Indian Head penny, too!"

She nodded. "Not many of them around any more."

Fifteen minutes later she slid on my socks and shoes, buckled my overshoes, and held my parka. She handed me my gloves, and placed the bag handle around my neck. She patted me on the back as I stepped out into the bitter cold again.

Over the next few years Chissie repeated the performance a couple more times on other deep-freeze days. As usual we chatted about coins, and sometimes she showed me arrowheads she and her husband John Ackerman – of "What's my name?" fame – had collected.

These kindnesses Chissie Ackerman and John showed me as I was growing up in Wishek were great gifts than I could never repay.

240

Collecting Bills

Pedaling around town with several thousand dollars stuffed in my back pocket did not seem unusual, even at twelve. Prove you were responsible, and age did not matter.

Though I did not feel emotionally safe in my life, I did not fear that a thief might be lying in wait behind the Nickisch building or a bandit in Ma's Dairy Queen lot to steal that cash as I moved through the streets. The town was safe.

It all came about when Fred Sayler, my stepdad's boss at Sayler Bros. Hardware, called me and said he wanted to see me. I trod up the steps into his office. He sat behind his desk in front of an open checkbook with large and long checks, three per page. They intrigued me.

He smiled and asked if I'd like to earn some extra money. I shrugged. I didn't want to empty freight trucks or wait on customers during summer vacation, and my mom and stepdad already assigned too many chores, so I prepared to say no. He didn't understand that all the money I earned from delivering newspapers or hauling bales or any other work was required to clink into the family's coffers, and not my pockets.

"What do you want me to do?"

"Collect bills. Walter says you collect hundreds of dollars for your paper routes, so this will be right up your alley. Interested?"

Because Walter worked for him, I didn't think I really had a choice. I glanced at his checkbook. He might pay me with one of those checks. That would be fun. So I nodded.

"Okay. Here's what you do." He opened a left-hand drawer and removed a sheaf of store bills with customer names at the top, and the amount below. "Show them the bill, and if they pay all of it, mark paid in full with your initials and the date, and hand them the bill. If they can't pay the entire bill, ask for five dollars. Or a dollar. Then mark that, the date and your initials, show it to them, and bring it back to me. Get something from everyone."

So I started collecting bills in June, many of them overdue, and again each first week of the month into November, rattling around town on my old Schwinn bicycle, and stuffing hundreds of dollars of cash and more checks into a brown pouch stuck in the back pocket of my jeans.

I also discovered what being poor really meant, people living in houses needing repairs, broken-down steps, peeling paint, people who reluctantly paid me five dollars a month on bills of fifty or a hundred, including parents of a few classmates who wore threadbare clothes and hand-me-down shoes – as I did. But their poor outdid mine by far.

I rapped on the door of one house whose husband spent too much time in the bar. The woman opened up a crack and peered out. The smell of whiskey and stale beer and poop flowed out, and I staggered back.

In one arm she held a snot-nosed baby sucking on a bottle; in the other arm fussed a twin half-dressed in a stained sweater. Neither wore a diaper. A dirty-faced urchin clutched each of the woman's legs, another grabbed her dress, and a pair two years older gathered behind her, their round faces gazing up at me like wilted flowers searching for the sun.

One look at her sorrowful face, the kids with ketchup on their patched clothes, the battered and broken toys strewn on the floor amidst dirty laundry, and I took pity. I asked if she could pay a dollar on their $15 bill, six months overdue.

She looked relieved. "Yes," she said. "I can." She delved into the bosom of her faded torn dress and triumphantly produced a crumpled greenback. I took it and wrote the payment and initial and date down on her slip, and showed her the new total. Tears filled her eyes. She merely nodded.

Each month after that we reenacted a similar scene, and I could see she was grateful to see the number diminish.

After collecting the November bills, Fred paid me with another large-sized paper check, which tickled me. Thus ended my bill-collecting adventures for Sayler Brothers. But my appreciation increased for how we lived – not perfect – but much better than some others in town.

Comics Libraries

I read truckloads of comics during my growing-up years. We had no extra money for fripperies like new comic books, so short of stealing them I needed to borrow them from somewhere. A comic library, if you will, to provide enough copies to keep me sated and happy.

Luckily, I did have a comic library. Or two, actually. First was Wiest Drug Store. Even in winter, about once a week I rattled my bike three blocks up to the store, which was filled with exotic figurines on glass shelves, alien scents swirling in the air, and a magazine rack.

I dallied by the figurines, examining one or two, acting like I was interested in them, causing the owner, Eugene Wiest, to frown, because some were expensive. If I dropped one, who would pay for it? I rifled through the record albums, edging toward the magazine rack, keeping a wary eye on Mr. Wiest behind the pharmacist's counter. When he turned his back to work on a prescription, I grabbed a couple of comics I had zeroed in on, and I plopped onto the floor behind the rack, out of sight. Sighing with satisfaction, I sat cross-legged, and started reading.

While faint footfalls of customers trod around me, I lost myself in the fantastic stories. In my mind I became each of the superheroes: Superman battling Lex Luthor, crime and deadly kryptonite; different members of the Justice League of America tackling foes; the Lone Ranger doing good with Tonto; and Batman fighting fiends alongside Robin. But not insipid Archie or Jughead.

I didn't realize that Mr. Wiest knew what I was doing. And I wasn't the only kid he allowed to read comics. Occasionally he might angle to observe me from behind the counter, eyeing me sadly. I could read a couple before I had to get back to chores at home.

Mr. Wiest occasionally handed me a stack of comic books without covers, to keep. They were still eminently readable. He had stripped the covers to send them back for credit as unsold.

The second library consisted of other kids in town. When I was running low I called someone who had a plethora of comics and said, "Do you want to trade?" I was always surprised when they sounded irritated, saying, "Trade what?"

"Comics, of course" I said. I figured when they heard "trade" they'd understand what I meant. I mean, we never traded bikes or marbles or stamps or anything else besides comics.

Comics could only be traded by following certain rules: regular comics with covers or without covers traded one for one, regardless of age; double-thick comics with covers traded for another double-thick comic, or two regular comics with covers; double comics without covers traded for two regular comics without covers.

In that way I gathered comics that excited me so much that I tried to squeeze them in during the day. If not, sometimes I read under bedcovers with a flashlight. That made my helping Superman even more thrilling!

Getting so involved with superheroes carried over into other comic stories. One comic I traded for had a story that haunted me, of a man who invented a potion that made him immortal, just as nuclear war broke out all around the world, (a very real possibility at the time) the pages full of atomic bombs exploding, killing everybody on earth.

Except Mr. Immortal, who couldn't die. He lived in a cave, where giant birds found him and pecked him apart bit by bit, until the last panel of the comic book showed only his red heart remaining. Still beating. I imagined myself the only person--or part of a person--still surviving.

Nevertheless, I kept getting comics from my local libraries, and reading them.

The Joy of Reading

While I was inside my mother's womb, she read from
the *Big Book of Fairy Tales* to my brother Bob – and me. The
sound of her soothing voice was music echoing in the dark
of my half-formed brain, and doubtless helped inculcate in
me the love of stories, and reading.

As I attended school, stories about Dick and Jane
seemed pretty thin gruel compared to Rumpelstiltskin
stamping so hard that he disappeared into the floor; or
Rapunzel letting down her long hair for the king's son to
climb into her tower; or the king marching naked.

Luckily, many days my elementary school teachers
read stories aloud. But as I became a more astute reader, I felt
unfulfilled. I hungered for stories that I chose to read. So
Mom got me a library card, and I began reading books to
delirium.

Happily I began pawing through the novels on the
shelves at the library, where I became acquainted with Edgar
Rice Burrough's Tarzan books (*Kreegah bundolo!,*) John Carter
on Mars, as well as the Hardy Boys adventure series. *The Secret
of Wildcat Swamp* was my favorite because it involved
paleontology, or fossils, which was in my blood. Meanwhile
Frank and Joe nabbed train robbers and a convict, and I felt
like I was their assistant.

Yet I could only check out one book a week every
Saturday. Unsatisfying, but I had to make do.

Until fifth grade when Scholastic Book Club came to
the rescue, offering a wide range of novels. After reading
Jules Verne's *Mysterious Island*, and *20,000 Leagues Under the Sea*,
I realized I loved science fiction.

The books in the club folder in school varied in
difficulty, but I chose what interested me. A couple of times
Miss Smiley said, "Are you sure you can read these books?"

I was surprised, because I was an excellent reader, and
she knew it. I said, "Sure."

But I felt insulted. Eventually I realized she probably thought, based on my hand-me-down clothes, floppy-soled shoes, stubby pencils, lack of a pencil box, and other missing items that other classmates had, that we couldn't afford the books. I couldn't blame her. With five voracious boys, our family had to be practical, and frugal.

But she didn't know I had begun delivering newspapers. Though all my profits were supposed to be deposited into the family coffers, Mom and Walter didn't know how much money I made, so I skimmed some off for books and bags of black Nibs.

The police station is at the steps on the left.

For a while I was satisfied with the new reading arrangements. But soon the extra two or three books a month were not enough to slake my insatiable reading habit. I wracked my brain, and came up with an answer: steal books from the town library!

Not really steal, but borrow – because I knew I wouldn't keep the books. I would always return them. Shouldn't be too difficult.

Nevertheless I was worried. The police station and jail were in the same building as the Wishek Library.

That made me nervous. What if I got caught? All the librarian had to do was yell, and the police would rush in with handcuffs. I wasn't sure of the prison sentence, and I certainly couldn't ask anybody, "Say, how long would I spend in prison if I was caught stealing library books?" That would give everything away.

Even so, I decided to take my chances. One Saturday after checking out my lone book, I sauntered back to the Hardy Boys' shelf and grabbed another mystery I had set aside. After paging through it, I tucked it under my arm, touched the spines of other books, and "absentmindedly" headed toward the door. Wow! Easy!

Until the librarian cleared her throat. "Billy!"

Whoops! The police slapped the handcuffs on and shoved me rudely inside the jail cell, chains clinking on my wrists as the heavy metal door clanged shut. Helplessly, I clutched the cold steel bars in my hands.

Or so I feared as my imagination ran amok with the librarian glaring at me. After a moment she said, "Billy, you know stealing isn't right. Now put it back."

I did, and showed her my only book was the one I had checked out. I turned to leave.

"Just a minute," she said. I turned around. "Promise me you won't do it again." She stared at me. "Promise?"

"Okay," I said meekly, "I promise."

"Okay then."

So that wasn't going to work. Seemed I was destined to spend my life without enough reading material.

The Library Card Caper

For a few weeks after being reprimanded I pondered possibilities for obtaining more books, but came up blank. Until one day I realized the answer was right in front of me all the time. More library cards! Hooray!

Of seven members in our family, only Ron and I read library books. That meant five cards remained unused, including those of my very young brothers! Soon my smile spread wide as an open encyclopedia as I found myself the proud recipient of six library books per week.

I was in reading heaven. I raced through books by Isaac Asimov, *The Caves of Steel,* and Ray Bradbury's *Fahrenheit 451, Martian Chronicles,* and *The Illustrated Man* – all of which lured me into their vivid empires with powerful amulets that felt like they could lead to paths of wisdom. They practically knocked me out.

Books transported me out of the everyday world and into new and mysterious and dangerous ones. I read books until I was delirious, ignoring my known world every possible moment, much to my parents' dismay. Too often my stepdad yelled, "Get your nose out of that damn book! There's work to be done!"

But when school let out, the book club ended, curtailing my books while increasing my reading time. Trading comics with friends helped, but I still required more books. Nobody in town sold the paperbacks I wanted, so I needed to figure out another way.

Which happened by accident. I lost my Billy Vossler library card, so I got a new one. A week or so later I found the lost one. My eyes opened wide. Without trying I had added one more card to my total. Seven books a week! This was more like it.

With larceny in my soul, I realized the answer to my problem: "lose" other family cards one at a time and get duplicates. Ten, eleven, twelve cards! The sky was the limit! I had promised that I wouldn't steal books – this was only borrowing. I'd return them.   But the caper ended quite suddenly one Saturday when I piled eight books on the librarian's desk, and realized she was a substitute. If I had paid attention earlier, I could have claimed that I had lost Mom's card. Maybe Bob's too. She wouldn't know the difference. Or challenge me. For a moment I considered returning two books to the shelves, saying I'd lost those two cards. But the books lay on the desk in front of her, and grabbing two and returning them would be awkward and suspicious. Plus she already had my pile of cards.

"You sure like to read, huh!"

"I do," I nodded. She frowned at the last book, picked up my pile of cards, sorted through them, and stopped. She held up four cards, looked at me, and said, "These cards are the same."

Uh oh. A problem. But I could solve it.

"Two have your name on them, two your brother's name."

"Oh," I said. "An accident, I guess."

She blinked and pursed her lips. "And now I think of it, your brother, I just checked out books for him an hour ago. He took five books, I think it was." She checked. "Yes, five."

"What?" I said, astonished. "But he couldn't..."

She frowned. "How many in your family? Five boys and your parents, right?"

I nodded. "Seven," I said with a sinking feeling.

She counted my books. "Eight for you and five for your brother makes thirteen." Unlucky thirteen I was now thinking. "Do others in your family have five cards or seven cards? Does your family have maybe a hundred cards?"

"Um, no," I said in a meek voice.

"So why does your family have thirteen cards?" She looked at me. "That we know of."

"Um," I said. "We like to read, I guess. A lot!"

"Uh huh. Ronnie used a card with your name..."

"Mine?" My mouth dropped open.

"So that makes three Billy Vossler cards." She glared at me. "You think it's fair for you to have three, and your family thirteen?"

"Um, I guess not," I said.

She lectured me about the limited number of books in our small library, and by taking twelve books a week, we were stealing books from others who like to read. "Is that fair, Billy?"

"Um, no, I guess not."

"Okay. So your brother took five books, and if I remember right, they were you boys' names." She checked the book-name cards in the file box. "Yes. So…" She picked up six of my cards, and slowly tore them into pieces, one by one. My heart sank. "Now, choose two books from your pile of seven, because you only have two legal cards."

I was aghast. "But…"

"No buts, Billy. You and Ronnie will have to figure out which cards each of you is going to use. And only seven altogether. Only one for each member of your family. Understand?" I nodded. "And it would seem to me that you would want to use your own card as one of them."

She tossed the shards of what had been my entry into extra books every week into the wastepaper basket beside her desk, and my heart fell. She said she would inform the main librarian about the situation. My heart sank even further. Maybe I would never be allowed to check out books from the library ever again?

Turns out, I could. The next time I saw the main librarian she gazed at me kind of funny, but didn't say anything. I checked out three books that week, and Ron four, and we alternated every week after that.

Not enough books, but honest ones.

Return to Woehl Stadium

One June day in my forties, clutching an ancient glove with a baseball tucked in its pocket, I made a pilgrimage to the stadium we built when I was in my early teens.

Three decades since I'd seen Woehl Stadium! Holding a photo with a curled edge, I shuffled through the matted outfield grass toward the listing backstop and the collapsed dugout, a surge of memories welling up – hitting home runs, fielding hard-hit balls, throwing strikes, flinging out baseball lingo, like "We want a pitcher, not a glass of water," or "Hum chucka baby!"

I looked at the photo, several of us standing near second base, bats laid against our shoulders with gloves looped over them. We are leaning against each other in an acceptable show of that powerful friendship which comes to most males only once in their lifetimes, during junior high. We are all dreamy-eyed, in the midst of that one perfect summer of playing baseball.

With my foot, I poked in the *marravarich* weeds for second base, the pitcher's mound, home plate. Then I heard rustling behind me, and an angry voice cried, "Hayyyy! You get out of here. Right now! Haaay!" He said again. "G-g-g-go away!"

I turned, and a stooped old man with white hair, wearing an engineer's cap, hobbled towards me, glaring. He brandished a bat, and held a ball in his stiff mitt.

For a moment I was taken aback. Then I said, "Ervin! It's me. Bill!" The fire of time had left only ashes of the man he had been.

He stopped. His rheumy eyes widened, and a great smile creased his lined face. "Biddee!" he choked, "Biddee! Yah, Biddee," grasping my hand like a lifeline. "But do you remember the time I hit a home run off you? Hee hee hee."

"Yeah, Ervin," I said, slipping an arm around his shoulder. "I remember." We walked for a moment, arms around each other's shoulders, the comfortable cloak of long-ago friendship slipping over us once again as we surveyed the ruin of years. "And do you remember. . .?"

"Oooh, I remember!" he interrupted, his eyes widening. He covered his crotch with a hand. "You hit that one good! Hee hee hee. You hit that one good, Biddee."

As we neared home plate, Ervin became agitated. "Yah, but Biddee," he said in a sad voice, "You don't come back. Don't you remember? 'Always friends, always together.'" He raised a finger in the friendship salute, and I raised mine too, tears filling our eyes. "You said that. I remember. Why don't you come to visit me?"

His words burned my heart. In my busy life, I rarely ever thought of Ervin, even though I'd learned a lot about life from him. I hung my head.

During the long silence, I struggled with tears. Finally I shrugged, and in a whispery voice said, "Even though I haven't come home in a long time, I come back here at Woehl Stadium with you, Ervin. Anytime I want. Up here." I touched my temple. "Or with this photo," which I showed.

"Ooh," he said, "Randy and Jim and me. Yah but Biddee, sometimes I walk over here and stand. And and and I see us playing baseball." His eyes were far away. "You and me and Ronnie and Randy and Jim, playing baseball. Up here." He pointed at his head. "I see us, too."

My eyes were moist. I hugged his wide sturdy shoulders, and we embraced fiercely. "Me, too," I said, muffled, "Me, too."

After a moment I took his bat, feeling its good cool smoothness in my hands, and walked toward home plate. I scuffled with the toe of my wingtips, and cleaned it off.

I turned, and motioned Ervin toward the pitcher's mound. His eyes lit up.

"Hum chucka! Chuck it in here, baby," I said. "We don't have forever to get ready for Yankee tryouts, do we?"

"Or or or D-d-d-Dodgers," Ervin said as he slowly wound up.

CPSIA information can be obtained
at www.ICGtesting.com
Printed in the USA
JSHW020811131022
31617JS00007B/170

9 798985 435511